DIANA'S DREAMS

DIANA'S
DREAMS

JOAN HANGER

JOHN BLAKE

Published by John Blake Publishing Ltd,
3, Bramber Court, 2 Bramber Road,
London W14 9PB, England

www.blake.co.uk

First published in hardback in 2005

ISBN 1 84454163 0

British Library Cataloguing-in-Publication Data:

A catalogue record for this book is available from the British Library.

Design by www.envydesign.co.uk

Printed in Great Britain by Creative Print & Design (Wales)

1 3 5 7 9 10 8 6 4 2

Papers used by John Blake Publishing are natural, recyclable
products made from wood grown in sustainable forests.
The manufacturing processes conform to the environmental
regulations of the country of origin.

CONTENTS

INTRODUCTION

'The whole dream work is essentially subjective, and a dream is a theatre in which the dreamer is himself the scene, the player, the prompter, the producer, the author, the public and the critic.'

CARL GUSTAV JUNG

DREAMS are messages from the wellspring of your deepest self. They allow you to tap into your intuition. You can ignore the messages from your dreams or you can allow your dreams to guide you to a deeper understanding of yourself, your relationships and your life.

This was something that Princess Diana was well aware of and she took a keen interest in the interpretation of her dreams. As she knew, dreams have been revered as useful messages throughout history. They were interpreted as signs from the world beyond death and sometimes they were thought to be premonitions.

In ancient times, Aristotle said dreams were indicative of man's connection to nature and himself. In recent history, dreams were the key to the discovery of the unconscious and the birth of psychoanalysis. Sigmund Freud wrote *The Interpretation of Dreams* in 1899, in which he linked dreams with underlying psychological states. He used dreams to analyse the underlying problems of his patients. Carl Gustav Jung, who studied with Freud, took these findings many steps further. He expanded the study of dreams to include complex symbolic patterns that shed light on the events of the dream. Both Freud and Jung agreed that interpreting dreams needed the input of the dreamer to work out what they really meant.

Today, much headway is being made in the study of dreams as scientists further explore the nature of the psyche. With the increasing complexities and demands of modern life, it is essential that we accept the messages that our dreams convey. It is important for all dreaming souls to watch and interpret the signals from their unconscious that link them with their deepest selves.

Princess Diana acted as a touchstone for our deepest yearnings and desires. Her dreams told her – and now can tell us – much about the deeper workings of the human psyche and its drive for happiness and fulfilment.

I met Diana a number of times and spoke with her on other occasions about her life and dreams. Dreams were the reason I met her. I had been commissioned to write a book on children's dreams. Part of the proceeds of the book were to go to the children's charity Barnardo's, Australia, and, as Diana was patroness of that charity, I had an idea that I would approach her to write a foreword, which she generously agreed to do.

Before my first meeting with Diana, I was very nervous. It took place at her private suite in Kensington Palace. She greeted me warmly like a friend. I followed her into a magnificent lounge, which was dripping with orchids and with the faint sound of classical music.

She asked me what I would like to drink and I said, 'I feel like I need something strong, as I can't believe I'm here with you.' It broke the ice.

She said, 'I don't drink, thank goodness, or else I'm sure I would be all over the newspapers as an alcoholic!' We laughed and the butler, Paul Burrell, proceeded to bring in a tray of coffee. It was exciting to be close to Diana. She was so energetic, yet quiet and elegant, so friendly and so feminine. She had a captivating presence that I felt as soon as she warmly took my hand. I felt her tremendous positivity but at the same time I could sense her fragility and great spirituality.

On reflection, after this first encounter I realised that I had gone to our meeting expecting everything about her to be perfect, formal and maybe even a little stiff. But the most delightful surprise was that she was so natural.

Diana dreamt vividly and remembered her dreams well. They were bridges between the reality of life as a princess, in the full glare of the public eye, and her deepest desires, insecurities and intuitions. We spoke animatedly about how to unravel their meaning. She wrote a most wonderful and spontaneous foreword for the children's dream book.

Apart from our meetings, we spoke from time to time on the telephone, especially if a dream was worrying her. Mostly, her calls were on a weekend when she had more time to herself. Of course, she would always have my undivided attention.

When I first conceived the idea for this book and talked about it to others, many had tears in their eyes as they talked about her. I received a large number of letters from those who loved her and dreamt about her in the course of my work as a columnist for the *Daily Mirror*. They also reported dreams about her death, not dissimilar to ones that occur after a global disaster of some nature. I had already written five books on dreams and it seemed to me that talking about Diana's dream-life – as she was such a dreamlike, ethereal figure in so many people's lives – would allow readers to connect with their own dreams in a very special way.

This is also a personal account of how Diana changed through the years, overcoming the trials and tribulations that we all face at some time or another in our lives. I've included dreams from my readers that show how much Diana was just like the rest of us – however, in her case, she had to play out all her adult experiences in the glare of the public eye.

I am often asked, 'Do you dream about Diana? Does she come to you in your dreams?' My answer is 'Yes, she does, and I love it.' I must say that I tend to look for her in my dreams.

Many others do too, though there can be few who have had such a chilling experience as the Sheffield housewife who told her pastor of a dream of Diana she had in May 1997. In it she saw someone standing by her bed. The person said, 'I am at work in the hearts and spirit of the people of this nation,' and went on to declare that the proof of the statement would be provided in 'a day soon when the whole nation will mourn and the whole nation will put flowers in their cities.' Three months later, Diana was gone.

I was devastated to hear the news of her death. I had spoken to her just a few weeks previously, when she was about to leave on a tour to publicise her campaign against landmines. I was hunted out on that unforgettable day by the media to comment on her death. I remember that I was in a state of shock and felt that it was not me talking, but someone else. Without the help of two beautiful friends, George and

Stephen, who supported me all day and into the night in television and radio studios, I think I would have collapsed. Privately, I asked myself who was I to comment? I couldn't believe that it was true.

It wasn't until I visited Westminster and the Princess Diana Foundation a couple of years after her death, when I once again met up with dear Paul Burrell, that I was able to come to terms with the loss. We talked of her and it seemed to me that it was my grieving time – I was able to face up to her death after talking to her 'rock' and my friend. And if this book is found on a bookshelf or on a bedside table then, in some small way, I will have fulfilled my dream for Diana.

Joan Hanger, August 2005

CHAPTER 1

PRINCESS IN WAITING

*'We are such stuff as dreams are made on; and
our little life is rounded with a sleep.'*
WILLIAM SHAKESPEARE, *THE TEMPEST*

WHEN Diana's sister, Lady Sarah Spencer, ended her liaison with Prince Charles, she is said to have commented, 'I am not the one for him, but I know who is. My sister Diana is only 16 years old, but she would be perfect for him.' Three years later, in 1980, Lady Diana Spencer began appearing by Prince Charles's side. She was 19 years old. Some of the press publicly wondered what 32-year-old Charles was doing, stepping out with a teenager. The shy kindergarten teacher was quickly dubbed 'Lady Di' by the media, immediately becoming public property – whether she was ready for it or not.

She was displayed, put on parade and openly assessed for her suitability to be Prince Charles's bride. It was the world's must public job interview. At least, that's what it must have felt like. The lovely Lady Di was never really wooed by her Prince Charming. For Charles, his relationship with Diana was a good piece of business for the family firm. Their engagement was announced with brisk efficiency and, later, as the big day itself loomed, Prince Charles began his wedding week by disappearing off to lunch with old flame Camilla Parker Bowles. Even before they had exchanged wedding vows, the tone of Charles and Diana's marriage was set. Diana knew or certainly suspected that Charles and Camilla's relationship had not ended but she was trapped – she could not withdraw from the wedding of the century – she would go through with it!

THE ROMANTIC TEENAGER

Diana grew up reading books by the romantic novelist Barbara Cartland. Diana didn't know that, by the time she was 16, Cartland would become her step-grandmother – in 1976,

Diana's father, the 8th Earl Spencer, married Cartland's daughter, Raine, Countess of Dartmouth. It was both parties' second marriage. To call Barbara Cartland a romantic novelist is an under-statement. Her books presented an idealised, almost fairy-tale, view of romantic love. Diana loved Cartland's books. She said that when she was growing up she dreamt of being loved and looked after by the man she married, just like in a Barbara Cartland romance.

We talked about Barbara Cartland, her flamboyant pink outfits, her larger-than-life personality. Diana had a fund of stories about her. She commented wryly that her marriage would not have looked out of place in a Cartland novel. 'Wouldn't my life now make a real love triangle!' she said.

It was during this conversation, in May 1996, that Diana shared her thoughts about a dream she'd had as a teenager: 'I wake up in a place that is quietly beautiful, like a magic garden. There are even sounds that you hear on a hot summer's day, like a bee buzzing. All around me the colours of the flowers are very bright and I feel as if I have just awakened from a sleep on the cool grass. I get up and walk around and find a little bridge and a stream under it and across the bridge is a field of blackberries. I remember saying to myself, "Blackberries, are they supposed to be in season now?" Somewhere, I find a little bucket and decide to go picking the delicious-looking blackberries, but as I try to enter the field where they are growing I notice a fence which seems to be at first too difficult for me to climb. But somehow I go around it and start tasting the blackberries. They were divine and I always remember this dream when I see them anywhere. As I decide to go back with my berries I notice a small little child in the garden playing with a toy spade. The child is a little boy and I seem to know that he belongs to me. What do you make of my teenage dream?'

I replied, 'I think it is a very typical dream that we have at that time of our lives. At that age, we live without worries and only think of a wonderful future, no matter what is going on around us. The delicious blackberries were your sexual feelings rousing and I think that the fence symbolised the restraints on you

4

because of your age. But you proved that you could get around it. The little boy that you felt drawn to was your longing to have someone of your own that belonged to you. You did eventually have that boy, of course, and another one. I think this was a positive dream in every sense and it also showed how you would enjoy your sexuality in the future.' I then concluded, 'The sounds were interesting in your dream, too, because we should never neglect sounds as they are related to our mystic qualities and our inner wisdom. I think these peaceful sounds indicate that your sexuality can be deeply satisfying to you at a spiritual level.'

Diana accepted this interpretation. She told me, 'What a pity you hadn't been around me when I was having those dreams.'

I told her that, even though I hadn't been with her at the time, the dreams had played a positive role in carrying Diana forwards. I reassured her that I was there for her now, and would help in any way I could.

It occurred to me later that Diana's memory of this dream had probably been triggered by the brave face she had to put on for the annual parents' day for Prince William at Eton. Diana had wanted to go with Prince Charles, as a couple, but as the parents' day was taking place virtually on the eve of their divorce her request was turned down. Only other divorced or separated mothers can have any idea how Diana felt as she stood there alone, watching her son, surrounded by happy parents and families. How she must have struggled to cover up her discomfort and disappointment.

Sexual-awakening dreams

It is important to remember that during REM sleep – which is when we dream – our sexual organs show all the signs of stimulation, even if we are not dreaming about sex. In adolescence, when we first 'wake' to our sexual desires, sexual dreams may result in wet dreams in boys and orgasm in girls. Some adolescents find themselves dreaming of having intercourse with their father, brothers, mothers, sisters or other relatives. Though unsettling, this is actually quite normal, as it depicts the unconscious connecting up of our earliest intimacies with the intimacies that will come in our adult lives. In most cases, these sorts of dreams at this age are quite healthy. Sexual-awakening dreams are often accompanied by images of fecundity – fruit, flowers, babies, streams, lushness. These are deeply symbolic of the burgeoning sexual life of the dreamer.

Q: In my dream I am travelling in the open on top of a double-decker bus. We were climbing a hill. I felt there were other people on the bus and the feeling was one of closeness and warmth. My little white poodle was following the bus, the same way that he follows us at home, and I could see him on the curve of the road. I chuckled and thought, 'He's always following me!' There was a tree overhanging the bus. I saw it was a date tree, although it did not look like a traditional date palm. The tree was bursting with fruit. The fruit resembled large plums that were a shimmering whitish blue. They were very juicy and, although juice dribbled down my chin and on to my fingers while I ate one, it did not appear to be sticky, and no one else noticed. Some of the fruit on the tree appeared to be wrapped in gold leaf and these were more elongated in shape, though they still retained their plumpness. The bus seemed to stop at this point and I regarded the tree as mine even though I did not pick the golden fruit. I just basked in the joy of it all. I felt at one with the Universe and woke up happy and relaxed and even sexy!

AMY, HERTS

A: Being in the open bus represents a new adventure for you and the message from your dream is that your taste for ripe succulent fruits, in different shapes, is associated with your sexual desires. You showed character by not gorging on the forbidden fruit from your hanging tree, yet you were quite comfortable in not thinking about what anyone else on the bus might think of you enjoying yourself so much. You even had your poodle following you, which caters for your comfort zone. The ripeness and juice from the fruit depicts your readiness for maybe your first sexual encounter and I am sure you have the power to really get 'stuck into it' and enjoy!

Q: Not long ago I dreamt that I was having a shower when my older brother came into the bathroom and the water turned so hot that it burned me. He then pulled me out of the shower, threw me on the floor and began raping me. The bathroom door was slightly open and I could see my parents in the next room so I started screaming out for them to help me – but they didn't! I have had this and similar dreams quite a few times. What do they mean?

WENDY, NOTTING HILL, LONDON

A: Sibling rivalry is one of the reasons behind a dream like this. You saw yourself as the victim in a dream at a time when your sexuality was defining itself. Rape in a dream can signify that you have been taken advantage of in some area of your life. The most telling part of your dream is your attempt to get your parents to help you in the face of your brother's power and dominance, and their lack of response. It may be a good idea to talk to them about this. Your dream shows that you are experiencing a natural stage of development.

SHY DI

When Diana first arrived at Buckingham Palace, prior to her engagement to Prince Charles, she was as unfamiliar with the royal family and their world as they were with her. She was ill at ease and shy – in fact, one of the nicknames she was given by the public was 'shy Di'. In contrast to her later reputation as a fashion icon, she arrived at the palace, according to former royal butler Paul Burrell in his book *A Royal Duty*, with a very inadequate wardrobe, ill-prepared for palace social events. Even the maid who was sent to help her unpack remarked on Diana's meagre clothing collection. She really didn't have a thing to wear!

When the announcement was made of Charles and Diana's engagement, on 24 January 1981, the media was allowed into the palace to photograph and film the happy couple. It's odd to think that the outfit Diana was immortalised wearing that day – her famous bright-blue skirt and collarless jacket, and white high-necked blouse – didn't even belong to her. After a fruitless search through Diana's wardrobe for something suitable to wear, palace staff gave up and ordered in the outfit from a fashionable London boutique.

Despite this inauspicious start, Diana, of course, soon shed her 'shy Di' tag to emerge a much stronger – and impeccably dressed – woman. However, when we talked about this time in her life, Diana did confide in me that she had suffered many nightmares.

One such nightmare was that she was in a train station waiting for a train that never seemed to arrive. Diana explained, 'I felt so frustrated and I began to get angry, then suddenly the dream changed and I was on the train track and I had on very high heels – which, I might say, I wasn't very keen on because of my height – and the heel of one of my shoes was stuck in the track. It was so frightening because suddenly the train was about to arrive; I could sense it in the distance. The track began to rumble. I looked up and there was Charles and Pa [Prince Phillip] trying to extricate my shoe, but my foot just wouldn't come out of the shoe and the shoe wouldn't budge. As they were trying to rescue me, I woke up in a right royal state!'

I thought about this dream and said, 'This dream depicts you being "stuck" in a desperate situation. Luckily, your fiancé was there to help as well as your future father-in-law but their efforts were futile. You woke up without having been saved from the threatening situation. The message was that you did have Charles and his father to look after you but, nevertheless, you regarded your forthcoming marriage with a sense of growing dread. You knew that it was going to challenge you. Trying to dislodge your shoe and foot could be a mirror of you trying to disengage from your situation. Maybe. Only you know how difficult that period was in your life – and how exciting. You had fallen in love with a prince and you were about to marry into the most famous and exclusive family in the world!'

Diana replied, 'I came to Buckingham Palace so excited but very nervous. At that time I really was the "shy Di" the press thought I was. Even though I came from a privileged background, I had really been just a kindergarten teacher and I loved my flat and my freedom. It was more than a shock to deal with all the requirements of palace life. There was so much going on all the time. I had to forge a place for myself, somehow. And don't forget that, as soon as our engagement was announced, Charles went off to Australia for a month.

'The palace rigours and routines were so challenging and I was very intimidated. I remember thinking even that early that I would have to organise my "own" people there if I was to have any say in anything.'

Paralysis dreams

Experiencing paralysis in dreams indicates fear, anxiety and resistance to change. Are you in a rut? Do you have the sense of not being able to move forward in your activities? What habits are you unable to shift? In REM sleep, where most dreaming occurs, our motor functions are immobilised. This may be one reason for the paralysis image appearing. Heavy bedclothes have also been suggested, and some psychologists hold that continued dreams of paralysis point to the necessity of a change in diet.

Q: As a child I often dreamt of being on a railway track with a train approaching very fast. I would try to get out of the way but my body would not move. I always woke before the train got to me, but now, at 33 years of age, I am still having the same dreams of not being able to move.

MONIQUE, SYDNEY, AUSTRALIA

A: Feeling paralysed in your dream with the train approaching indicates that you are in a dead-end situation, either emotionally or physically. As the dream has continued into your adult life, I would say that you had better face up to a big change as soon as possible. It sounds like this has become a personality trait that is definitely holding you back. You need to take stock of how you approach your future. It's time to try a new you.

THE ENGAGEMENT

Another scenario Diana talked about after her train nightmare was a dream where her mother-in-law, the Queen, figured prominently.

She said that the scene took place in her kindergarten with her 'littlees', as she called the children she looked after.

'There were children in the play area and all the carers were there, too, including me. I was telling the children to line up as we had someone special coming to visit. I was about to go to the front of the line-up, when I saw my future mother-in-law coming out of the kitchen, wearing an apron. On her head she had a wonderfully glowing tiara. She was carrying a plate of fruit that had been cut up into small pieces. A child went past me and walked up to the Queen to get some fruit. The Queen held out her hand and gave the child a precious stone, which the child then gave to me. Each child went up in turn and the same thing happened every time. The stones were rubies, diamonds, emeralds and sapphires. As each child gave me a jewel, I put it in my jacket pocket and said "thank you". The colours were so vivid. I had this dream a couple of times. It was all so sweet.

'While the children were eating the fruit, the Queen secretly beckoned for me to follow her. We went around the side of the building and the Queen pointed to my finger and softly took my ring finger in her hand. I stood there puzzled and I did not protest in any way. She didn't speak but pointed to my pocket and I gave her my jewels. She nodded and quietly moved away. I woke up at a loss to understand why the Queen would be at my kindergarten wearing an apron. I did think about why the Queen would want more jewels. I am not a person that's mad for jewellery. I love what I love and I don't yearn for this ring or that bracelet, like some do. What can it mean?'

I asked Diana when this dream occurred and

she told me that it was around the time of her engagement.

I said, 'Jewellery in our dreams symbolises our sense of self-worth. As a girl who was about to become a princess, it was hardly surprising for you to dream about jewellery – jewels are part and parcel of royal dress and life.'

She replied, 'Joan, yes, I would have been only a few days away from moving into the palace when the engagement announcement was made. But why was the Queen in the dream?'

I explained to her that dreams often used a mixture of mundane symbols that can appear ridiculous on waking. I offered the explanation that the Queen was at the kindergarten as a symbol that Diana was about to leave that place – and that life – forever. As we discussed things further, Diana suddenly remembered something. She told me, 'I didn't go shopping with Charles for my engagement ring. The Queen chose my wedding ring. And what a lovely ring it was.'

'There you go,' I replied. 'No wonder your mother-in-law-to-be was in your dream. It was to show you that she was the matriarch and that she was in charge of handing out the Crown's jewels.'

'I love that, Joan!' laughed Diana.

Wedding dreams

If you are about to get married, dreaming of your wedding is pretty standard night-time fare. You may dream of many different scenarios – including those that express your anxiety, such as dresses falling off, grooms or brides not turning up, parents being absent or angry, or any number of issues that could upset the day. However, people who are already married can also dream of weddings. In this case, a wedding dream often suggests the union of opposite yet comple-mentary parts of the self, and the promise of future fertility. Dreams associated with weddings or other anniversaries can serve as reminders of transience, or more positively as indications of the significance of human and family ties, of the vows and undertakings associated with them, or – if the emotional charge is negative – of the restricting commitments.

Q: I am engaged to be married soon and I have had this dream a couple of times. I am walking down the aisle and everything looks beautiful, but as I walk along I look for a friend who isn't there. My little bridesmaids turn around and come back to me instead of walking in front and they pull at my dress; as I look down, they show me their little hands and there are large golden bands with sparkling diamonds around their wrists. I am happy but shocked and know I can't go on until my friend appears and tells me that it is the 'right' thing to do – get married! When I wake up, I always check my wedding finger for my band!

ALICE, SOUTHAMPTON

A: It could be that you have the pre-wedding jitters. You need to do some soul-searching – is this really what you want? – but put it in perspective at the same time. This sort of doubt affects many brides-to-be. It sounds as if the bridesmaids were children, which is a very good sign. They point to a loving, fertile (in all ways) relationship. The jewellery on their hands represents beauty and value, both of which you should have in abundance on your wedding day.

CHAPTER 2

PALACE PRESSURE

'The awful shadow of an unseen Power/Floats through unseen among us.'

PERCY BYSSHE SHELLEY, 'HYMN TO
INTELLECTUAL BEAUTY'

DIANA felt – and indeed was left – very much alone from the beginning. If she had a problem and asked for help from palace officials, they told her to work it out herself – her business was none of their business. She was naive and without experience either of handling the media that besieged her or of the rules that were imposed on her when she moved into the palace six months prior to her wedding. Prince Charles offered little help, either. He was often away. Diana survived by becoming very self-reliant. She played on her 'shy Di' persona to help her get through. Palace officials viewed her as quiet, unassuming and not very bright. But, while the royal family's courtiers sneered at her, Diana drew on her experiences at the palace. They gave her those senses of humility and humanity that would turn her into a truly effective communicator – and into the People's Princess.

PERFORMING IN THE PUBLIC EYE

Even though Diana would one day become a great communicator, truly able to touch people's lives, her dreams during the early months of her marriage show how anxious she was at the prospect of having to speak in public – something that is expected of every member of the royal family.

Her social vulnerability showed up when she described a recurring dream to me. Apart from a few details, the dream was the same each time. Diana was always in front of a large audience delivering a speech. In one particularly bad version of the dream, the audience began to throw things at her. Other variations on this dream were that a fierce wind blew all the spectators away; in another, the spectators all turned their backs on her. She felt mortified in these dreams and couldn't speak, holding her hands up in front of her face in a futile effort to protect herself.

'Did you feel that you had no voice, or that your ideas were not being listened to?' I asked her. I also advised her to keep practising her public speaking. She was certainly much better at it by the time I got to know her. She told me that her confidence grew each time she had to speak in public.

Diana was always being tested and it wasn't a surprise to hear her describe a dream on this theme. It was another recurring dream, which, as I explained to her, came back at times of stress and when she felt particularly vulnerable and isolated.

In the dream, she was back at school and surrounded by her former schoolmates. The dream was set around the time she was studying for her kindergarten teaching exams. She said she saw herself in front of three teachers who were asking her questions. She was unable to respond and just stared at them blankly.

I said, 'You were feeling that you had to pass a test in your everyday life. I am not surprised that you had this type of dream. It's very common. Many dreamers recount a feeling of inadequacy when they describe this sort of dream to me. The message from your dream is that you feel as though you are still being examined, that you need to prove something by passing a test set by the powers-that-be.'

She replied, 'Yes, I often felt as if I had broken some rule or something like that and these people were cross with me.'

I said, 'Well, if you felt as if you had misbehaved, then the message could be that you have a strong sense of rebelling against restrictions put upon you.'

'I can relate to that!' she said.

Exam dreams

Exams in dreams often indicate a high anxiety level in the dreamer, who is feeling that they need to perform in some way to gain approval or praise. The examiner or examiners in the dream represent a part of ourselves which is 'judging' our own behaviour or skills. Ask yourself what test you are being asked to pass in your life when you experience this sort of dream.

Q: I am at my old school desk sitting an exam with all my old mates around me, like a trip back into the past. I feel comfortable and then the feeling changes because I cannot seem to complete the exam paper.

DAMIEN, WEMBLEY, LONDON

A: This dream depicts humiliation at not being able to complete an examination paper. Society today demands that we are constantly examined or tested in some way. Fear of failure is common. Being unprepared for your assignments or work duties can cause this type of dream. Try to define what or who is testing you in your daily life. Work out what it was that you were not quite prepared for. It seems that life now is much more stressful for you than it was in the days when you sat at your old school desk. Try to reduce the pressure in whatever areas it is becoming troublesome.

Q: I am told by my boss to telephone someone and give them some important information. But in my dream I can never get through. I dial the number and no one answers. It rings and rings and I wake up feeling very stressed and worried.

JOHN, PHILBEACH GARDENS, LONDON

A: This is a variant of the exam dream. You are unable to complete a task that someone of authority has given you and so you become very anxious about your performance. It also appears that you are experiencing some sort of communication breakdown, as you are not able to get through on the telephone. Stop and take a deep breath and look at how you deal with your superiors and your workload. It sounds like you are taking on too much and not communicating your need for extra explanation and help.

THE SHADOW

Diana was worried by a dream where she was left with a strong feeling that someone was watching her through her window or from the garden. When she woke from this dream she was disorientated, and didn't know whether she had dreamt it or whether it was real. On waking, she rushed to the window to look out, but no one was there. It left her with a feeling of dread.

Diana said, 'Why would I feel this way?' and I replied, 'Security is paramount in your life. It is not something that you had to deal with before your marriage. You also told me that you felt unprotected from the negative forces around you – the palace officials and the press – and there's the dissatisfaction you feel about the way you think Charles failed to help and protect you.'

'Yes,' she said, 'but at the same time I wanted to be on my own two feet and free of "their" control.'

'Who are "they"?' I asked.

She said, 'Charles, and all the hierarchy.'

'Is this dream frequent? Have you had it often?' I asked.

'Yes, a few times at that time of my life, and it sometimes comes back, but rarely now,' she replied.

I went on. 'Did you feel as though you would meet the person who was observing you? Or did you want to meet this person in the dream?'

'No, it seemed that it was a silent watcher. I woke up with a start once, thinking he or she was near my bed,' said Diana.

'Well,' I said, 'I think this example is what we call in dream symbolism the Shadow dream. The silent sense of someone nearby is frightening yet it can be a message from your subconscious to take notice of the other side of your self – your own dark side – because you need this side of your self to help with what is happening in your life. I know we all think we are nice people, and not at all nasty, but we all have another side of self.'

Diana was surprised by this, but I continued, 'Didn't you think it obvious when you were awake that without the official palace security you were very much alone and a target where anything could happen to you?'

'I had my courage and my pride. I thought I could do it on my own,' she replied.

'Perhaps you can,' I answered, 'but your dream's message was strong because you had the dream more than once. I think the reason why this dream has abated is that you have learned how to deal with your darker, more powerful side. You are much more comfortable with your mature self, now. Also, on a lighter note, in relation to your dream, may I ask an impertinent question?'

'Yes, of course, what is it?' said Diana.

'Were you pregnant at any time when you had this dream?' I asked.

'No, Joan! Why did you ask that?' she said, smiling.

'Because an "intruder" figure in a dream can also depict a coming pregnancy,' I said.

'No way, Jose!' she said, and we both laughed.

Interestingly enough, when Prince Charles talked about Diana's developing eating disorders, he would apparently refer to them as 'her other side'.

Shadow dreams

One of the most important elements of dream analysis, the Shadow expresses all that we would like to forget or deny about ourselves. It represents our 'bad' side, including negative urges such as greed, lust, hate and violence. The force of these hidden urges can make the Shadow a very potent figure indeed when it appears in our dreams.

The Shadow appears frequently in bad dreams or nightmares. It can appear as a pursuer, a bringer of bad news or any other threatening figure. In whatever form, the Shadow is usually tied up with a feeling of fear, because accepting our own dark side can be extremely difficult.

For most of us, the Shadow appears in daily life as tantrums, spiteful or selfish behaviour, telling lies, drinking to excess, gossiping nastily or even eating that extra piece of chocolate that you know you shouldn't have. Our Shadow side is not necessarily evil, although repression can make it so. The Shadow is ultimately connected to our moral sense. It certainly takes a strong moral effort to examine oneself and recognise the dark aspects of our Shadow as real aspects of our conscious selves. It's all too easy to distance ourselves from our dreams in the cold light of day.

Q: In my dream I saw a hooded figure standing against a very dark background. I couldn't see its face. The figure moved as if to grab me; I felt it grab me and I screamed. As I woke, my husband was standing at the foot of the bed and he said I looked scared.

DEBBY, GLASGOW

A: The Shadow beside your bed represents your other self, trying to get in touch with you. We must all recognise that we have two sides of self; your black figure is faceless because you have not yet recognised this fact. Your dream produced fear, so try to work out what or who it was that was stopping you from showing what you really feel about a person or place.

CROSS-DRESSING

Diana was concerned by a strange dream where she saw herself dressing in a man's suit for a secret dinner. In her dream, she saw herself in the full outfit of a man: the suit, the tie, even the brogues. She laughed about it to me and remembered that when she awoke she couldn't stop laughing – but during the dream she didn't like it at all.

I said, 'The true meaning of any dream is related to the feeling you experience on waking. Laughing about your dream is great.' I continued, 'Is disguise important to you?'

Diana threw herself back in her chair and put both hands up to her face. 'I often go about disguised!' she exclaimed.

'Your dream was saying to you it was time for you to integrate your female side with your male side. Whether we are male or female, we all carry within us the "other side" of our personalities. It may have been a time when you needed to show your inner strengths, strengths that you didn't even realise that you had.'

'That's true enough,' she said, 'how often

have I needed to be "someone" I know I'm not.'

I said, 'Clothes are incredible symbols in our dreams; they can display positive signs of the side of ourselves we don't show in our everyday life. In dreams, unusual clothes also tell us that we have the power to make many choices about how we express ourselves. Seeing yourself dressed as a man pointed out your internal sense of authority and strength to deal with whatever challenges were coming your way.'

Diana replied, 'My dreams are becoming much clearer, or rather the messages from my dreams are making sense, especially after I talk with you. Yes, I know now that I have choices, that's for sure! Even though I used to think for years that I didn't.'

I answered, 'Our dreams are creative processes that can change the way we view ourselves, our relationships and our daily active world — they teach us to say to ourselves "Who am I?" Your dreams are more coherent because, through them, you are getting in touch with yourself.'

Cross-dressing in dreams

Dreams about cross-dressing may indicate hidden desires but are more likely to indicate an imbalance in regard to the gender-identification of the dreamer. Is your feminine/masculine side repressed or overactive? Are you disturbed by what your job or your associates require you to emphasise? How comfortable are you with the roles that your gender imposes? Dreamers often report feeling disturbed on waking from a dream in which they are enjoying intercourse with someone of the same sex when they are not homosexual. It may be that these dreamers need to engage more fully with their own feminine or masculine power, or with the power of their internal opposite.

Q: For many years now I've had a recurring dream that I am dressed in women's clothing. I wear a straight skirt, about calf length. Over this, I wear one or two ladies' bib aprons that fold around the entire get-up. I seem to feel great and comfortable and I always have a lot of people around me in various situations. No one seems to notice my unusual gear except myself. When I wake up I am appalled for I have no desire to realise my dream, not even in the privacy of my own home. I hope you have an explanation for me.

A: You should look at your dream with humour not self-disgust. As it is recurring, it would be interesting to note what happens on the day of the dream because it shows you being at home with your feminine side, which is very positive. The presence of other people who do not notice your garb supports this.

HIDDEN FORCES AT WORK

Diana once dreamt of receiving a parcel by post. In the dream, she looked at the back to see who had sent it to her. There was no return address. When Diana opened the brown paper parcel, she discovered a nest of red spiders inside. The spiders then turned into a basket overflowing with letters. She tried to push them back in but they wouldn't fit. She remembered that she had this dream several times before her infamous *Panorama* interview in 1995.

Diana loved writing letters and she loved receiving them, too. I have kept my letters from Diana and I loved how she always put a meaningful line under certain words that she wanted to highlight to me or emphasise.

It is interesting to note here that for Sigmund Freud the envelope represented a female sexual symbol in his dream analysis.

I interpreted Diana's dreams as representing her role as a receptacle for many people's secrets, as well as her own. I also thought of the hidden forces against her that she faced each day. She had mentioned one particularly offensive secret, which was the special telephone line that had been installed for Charles so that he could contact Camilla without fear of being taped.

I told her that spiders also symbolise responsibilities and that they are connected to universal forces because of their ceaseless work of building and destroying. As they were red spiders, I pointed out that this signifies aggression, energy, blood, anger and passion. Diana agreed: 'Well, Joan, I had to be passionate and also aggressive in my thoughts and plans for the future.'

I went on to say that I felt that her dream was prefiguring some of the enormous consequences that would result from the *Panorama* interview being broadcast – both positive and negative.

I said that I felt she needed to delegate more instead of trying to be the only one who could organise all her everyday duties. This made sense to Diana. In fact, at this time she was actively instructing her staff to take on more responsibilities.

These dreams had occurred before I knew Diana, but how appropriate they had been. Coming as they did before she took on the *Panorama* interview, they showed her how she needed to call on every ounce of her inner strength to help her to divulge the secrets of her marriage to the BBC. It was just after this historic interview took place that I first met Diana.

In another dream in the same vein – again, she remembered that she'd had it around the time of the *Panorama* interview – she tried to push some overflowing letters back into a basket. As she did so, they turned into three little bright-red Buddhas.

I thought the three little Buddhas interesting, as the teaching of Buddha is that truth is found from within. The number three was significant, too, as in Buddhism that number represents harmony and spirituality. 'What did these Buddha figures mean to you?' I asked.

She considered for a while and then said, 'I thought they were cute in my dream. In real life, although I admire all forms of religion, I don't follow any one in particular. Did these Buddhas have any significance for me?'

'Let's look at it again,' I said. 'Your dream started with a feeling of frustration but then the letters turned into Buddhas. I think that this dream indicates that your search for truth and trust will come to an end only when you discover your true spiritual identity.'

Recurring dreams

When a troubling dream returns to us over and over again, it indicates that the message is not being interpreted or confronted by the dreamer. I am often asked to comment on dreams that have plagued the dreamer from their childhood until late into adult life. Generally speaking, a dream of this kind is usually an attempt to compensate for a blind spot in the dreamer's attitude to life, or it may date back to a traumatic moment or event that has been left unresolved in the unconscious.

Frequently, after we examine and accept the emotional difficulty symbolised in the recurring dream, it ceases to occur. Dreamers often report that the recurring dream is exactly the same each time it is dreamt; however, on closer examination this is rare. Most commonly, a recurring sequence or significant symbol will occur in the wider context of a dream. If you are subject to a recurring dream, try to note down all the details each time it occurs. You may notice a progression or development in the nature of the symbols presented or the context in which they arise. This will give you a chance to reflect on where you stand in relation to the dream, psychically, each time it reappears.

Q: I always have dreams about being on a surfboard in the ocean and being attacked by sharks. I always seem to get to the shore somehow. These dreams puzzle me because I love the sea. What can they mean?

MALCOLM, BRIGHTON

A: You may love the sea, but if you are a surfer then your fears have at least a possible basis in reality. Being attacked in the ocean by a creature from the deep indicates you are feeling emotionally attacked. Ask yourself, what do sharks mean to you? As this is a recurring dream and you are subconsciously attuned to its recurrence, consciously visualise yourself fighting back. This may change the course of the dream the next time you have it. Remember that the shark is a predator and you must be wary of anyone in real life that may have predatory designs.

Q: I have a recurring dream that I am in a lift by myself. I push a button to go to the fortieth floor; the elevator takes off like a rocket, and I can hardly hang on. When I get to the top, I step out and have a look, get back in and push the button for the ground floor. Again, the lift takes off like a rocket and I can't hang on. My head keeps hitting the top of the lift.

SID, WATFORD

A: You are certainly experiencing some highs and lows! Is this happening in your everyday life? Can't you get it together? Examine your personal life or career; a strong desire is being depicted, but then returning to the ground. Dreams of out-of-control lifts or elevators are similar to dreams of falling. Who or what is in control, and why?

Q: In my recurring dream, my younger child is always lying face down in water, either a pool, a river or a beach. When I find her and lift her out of the water, she is always alive. This dream disturbs me greatly.

EVELYN, BRISBANE, AUSTRALIA

A: This type of dream is prevalent among mothers of young, growing children. Seeing a child drowning in a dream may reflect your fears about her stage of growth or independence. Death in dreams is really the ending of a stage, or completion. It is not necessarily death in actuality. Look back to your own life and try to remember if a similar situation occurred to you or your siblings. If you cannot swim, this could be a reason for the dread you feel. Naturally, security precautions should be a top priority if you have a pool.

CHAPTER 3

A TROUBLED SOUL

*'Our truest life is when we are
in dreams awake.'*
HENRY DAVID THOREAU

THE demands on Diana as HRH the Princess of Wales were enormous, made all the more so by her isolation from Prince Charles. She was disorientated and intimidated by Buckingham Palace and she felt closed in. Depression and mood swings developed more regularly as Diana tried to cope. Her depression became chronic and she became bulimic. Diana had shown signs of being excessively neat and tidy as a child and teenager, and the seeds of her insecurities were sown in her upbringing – her parents divorced in 1969, when Diana was just eight years old. After only a few months of marriage, in October 1981, Diana threatened to 'cut her wrists'. Prince Charles persuaded her to go to a clinic for help. She was prescribed Valium, which she rejected. Diana refused to admit that she was seriously ill.

EATING DISORDERS

Diana talked to me about many of the ghastly dreams that she had experienced during the time she was affected by bulimia.

In one of Diana's dreams, she felt she was in her own home but everything – items of furniture, windows and doors – were not as they should be in real life. Small items in the kitchen, such as the toaster or the kettle, were enormous. She felt overpowered by their size. She searched for food in the cupboards but could find none. All she found were cracked cups and plates. Suddenly, a group of strangers appeared, taking occupation of Diana's home.

I told Diana that I felt this dream possibly indicated her wish to be able to combat her bulimia with more confidence. As I didn't know her at the time she was having these dreams, I told Diana that, if she had been able to link everyday events to the dreams, it would have helped her condition. I said, 'Perhaps the cracked cups and plates represent what you saw as faults in your personality or even the loss of someone much loved.'

She said, 'Yes, you're right! I was so lonely and Charles had removed himself emotionally from me, even then. Actually, I don't think he ever bonded with me emotionally at all.'

When we dream about houses, the kitchen represents the place where we get our spiritual and emotional sustenance.

Another dream that she told me about from this period was one where she saw herself as extremely thin. She had this dream on a recurring basis. She saw herself trying on clothes from a pile and, as she chose a skirt or a top that she liked, it would simply fall off her body. They were all much too big. I explained to Diana that this dream had recurred regularly due to her condition at the time. I also asked her if she had been in the company of people who were demanding or overly possessive. She remembered that she was feeling lonely and suffocated by officialdom.

Carl Gustav Jung, the founder of analytical psychology, said that some dreams give very clear messages concerning both our physical and psychological health. Diana's dream could have been a source of help to her in her bulimic state. It was recurring and therefore the message from her subconscious was being ignored. She knew she was losing weight but didn't know what to do about it. She had 'lost' herself.

By the time I met Diana, she was definitely not bulimic. She was radiant with health. Her eyes were alive and bright and she was able to talk to me about that difficult period in her life with some degree of perspective. She described how she had been such a young and vulnerable person. But now I was looking at a confident and charming young woman. She wasn't 'shy Di' any more. In my opinion, she had 'run the course' and won, bulimia or no bulimia.

Dreams of eating or food

Food symbolises nourishment. Why, how and what are you consuming? Are you hungry or have you eaten to excess in your dream? Are the images of food associated with guilt or pleasure?

Eating is often connected with sexuality and sensuality: Freud suggests fasting and gorging depict our sexual desires. Fasting can be related to self-punishment, whereas if you overeat in a dream it often represents greed or short-sighted grasping behaviour. Eating with others could indicate aspects of social behaviour: if you feel uncomfortable, then this could be a sign of social awkwardness. Are you having difficulties feeding from and giving to the relationships around you? Similarly, spoilt or bad-tasting food could relate to emotional nourishment, indicating problems in regard to a primary relationship.

Fruits are traditionally recognised as obvious sexual symbols; chocolate signifies self-indulgence. Perhaps you need to indulge yourself more frequently.

Q: I dreamt that I was wearing a white long lacy silk dress. My hair was down to my waist. I was slim. I walked up the stairs like I was in a trance, either side of the stairs were columns of an old castle. When I got to the top, there was nowhere else to go. I looked back and the wind blew my hair about. I woke peaceful and also amazed, for I am overweight, not slim!

LEANNE, SYDNEY, AUSTRALIA

A: Your dream's message is a wish-fulfilment. It was sent to encourage you to become fit and climb the heights to a new you!

CHILDHOOD INSECURITY

Diana was a very fit person. She especially loved swimming and going to the gym, so I was surprised when she told me of a recurring nightmare she had suffered from as a child, where she couldn't walk or run anywhere and was only able to move in slow motion.

The setting for the dream was a hot summer day. Diana was standing alone on a long deserted road, with a heat haze shimmering in the distance. She could feel the sun blazing down upon her as she noticed a sinister figure running towards her through the haze. Diana felt that the figure was going to 'get' her; she tried to run away but found that she couldn't –

her legs wouldn't work. It was as much as she could do to slowly drag herself into the grass verge at the side of the road to hide, forcing her unwilling legs to move painfully slowly.

Then the scene changed and she was sitting on the back of a camel as it ate some grass. She dug her heels into the camel's side to make it walk but it wouldn't budge. Then, she slid off the camel and found herself running in slow motion from something or someone that was chasing her. She ran along a dark and dirty corridor, with big dusty windows that were too high to see out of, and into a room. The presence followed her in. With great effort, still in slow motion, she made it out of the room and slammed the door. She moved off again but when she turned around she saw a monstrous face and screamed. The scream woke her each time, and she would be tense and rigid in her bed and covered with sweat. Sometimes, her muscles would ache with the effort that she had expended in the dream.

'I don't know when I first had this dream,' she told me. 'Probably around ten or twelve years old, but even remembering it makes me feel heavy with anxiety.' Now that she was older,

49

Diana told me that she thought the message from this dream was that she was powerless when confronted with other people's hostility. I told her, 'That may have been the case when you were younger, but it's not how it is today, is it?'

I went through aspects of the dream with her. Her slow-motion running emphasised her sense of not being able to escape from hostility. The camel represented the natural force of her emotions that refused to take her along the road to a less threatening place. The long corridor was imprisoning and the high windows prevented her looking out to get a broader view on what was happening. However, she *was* determined in her desire to get away from the presence, and she was quite clever in trapping it (so she thought) in a room. I told her that this was one positive aspect of her dream – it showed her single-mindedness. I said, 'And your single-mindedness has stood you in good stead. You've certainly needed it, to show your strength both for yourself and for your boys.'

The ending of the nightmare was a confrontation with the terrible demon of her own insecurity. As a child, it must have been a truly awful experience – but I told Diana that I felt that she had courageously confronted it in her real life, and had won. She agreed but then furrowed her brow. 'But have I been my own worst enemy? Do I lead myself into all my own difficulties?' she asked.

'This is one of the great questions of life,' I replied. 'How much do we attract and reflect our own perceptions of the world? How much control do we really have? Our dreams have the power to make us think about what it is that we are really doing each day, and how our thoughts and actions affect how the world "treats" us. The most important thing about this dream is that it is in the past and that you have now developed much more strength and security as a person now.'

I felt that Diana had had a long battle to establish a healthy ego and to design her persona exactly as she wanted it to be.

Dreams of insecurity, persona and ego

Essentially, the persona is our mask. While society deems it necessary for us to present a cohesive face to the world, it is often at the risk of losing touch with other, equally important, elements of ourselves. 'A man cannot get rid of himself in favour of an artificial persona without punishment,' said Jung. When there is too much identification with the mask, usually there are negative compensations in private life: the classic example being the respectable husband who indulges in secret affairs and whose wife, unable to dislodge his mark of respectability, becomes sick, reclusive or mentally unstable. The persona is not subjective – that is, it is not produced from our impressions or intuitions or inner state. Rather, it is a useful objective tool developed by the ego in response to the requirements of the world, society and our ambitions. This in itself is not a problem: the persona only becomes problematic when it replaces the self in all its complexity. Then, the persona can become a tyrannical, rigid construct.

An overactive persona may give rise to dreams in which the dreamer appears naked, or is ostracised in some way.

Q: I have had this dream a few times and it really shocks me. I have a very good job as a private secretary and in my dream I am at work, dressed exactly as I would be usually but without my blouse. I am working away, doing my regular jobs, and nobody takes any notice of me. I am decked out with just a bra and skirt. The dream leaves me feeling very confused and embarrassed, as I am a very conservative person usually.

BRIONY, BIRMINGHAM

A: Your dream is opposite to how you see yourself and depicts you being exposed. Many dreamers see themselves partly clothed or naked. It represents a fear of being seen for what they really are. At work, you may cultivate the image of Miss Perfect. Do you have a secret wish to be seen as something else? Your dream is dramatising this sort of hidden dilemma between your persona and who you really are.

Q: My boyfriend and I are both putting up mirrors. I am putting up a little mirror and he is putting up a huge mirror. He is no help to me because his main occupation is putting up the largest of mirrors for himself. Then, in my dream, the two mirrors are sitting side-by-side. I spent all the time in my dream admiring my boyfriend and how he looked in his mirror. In the corner of the room, just looking on without a smile, was my mother; she was like an invisible person in the room. They didn't help me put my mirror up and that hurt me!

ELAINE, MANCHESTER

A: Your insecurity as to your own identity leads you to spend your time encouraging your boyfriend's ego in your dream. You regard yourself as having only a small ego – and you are resentful about this. It may be a childhood lack that has been fostered by your mother – hence her position in your dream. In struggling with your self-image, you seem to put the man in your life on a pedestal! It's time for you to build a big mirror for yourself and lavish your ego with love.

FEAR OF ABANDONMENT

Diana had a deep fear of being left alone or abandoned. This fear stemmed from her childhood, which was not exactly idyllic. She told me about the dreams that gave voice to this insecurity.

'I did dream about being left behind by my mother,' she remembered sadly.

I said, 'That's natural because you were left with your father when your mother departed the family home.'

She described the dream, which was recurring: 'There was an earthquake, a tidal wave or something that was about to endanger our lives. Someone offered to take us to safety, but there was only room for one of us. My mother went with this person and left me behind.'

'You had a heartbreaking sense of being abandoned by your mother,' I said. 'What made it worse was that this dream kept recurring and you had no one to share your worries with.

Not only was there a theme of abandonment in your dream, but there was a threat of a catastrophe, too, something overwhelming. What was happening in your family at the time is presaged in this dream. You had a need to be rescued but the sad thing is that, somehow, you didn't expect to be. It is not surprising that these dreams left you feeling depressed – and that you still feel that way when you remember them now. You told me that you used to regularly visit your mother and have happy times with her, but it's often hard for a child to communicate complicated emotions to a parent. I wish I had been around to help you because I do believe you needed counselling at that time.'

Diana agreed and added, 'Yes, that would have been ideal because I always hid my feelings from my father, as I didn't want to upset him.'

On another occasion, Diana was about to leave on a royal visit and she told me she had had a dream about being in an exotic foreign palace. She said it was a peaceful place covered in marble, with tall, strong pillars that were somehow significant. The palace was empty.

She was the only person there. Then the dream changed and the atmosphere was that of a busy, historic square, like St Mark's Square, in Venice. There were lots of people bustling around, talking, walking and going about their daily business.

She said she felt so alone in this dream. In the first image, she was literally alone; in the second, no one noticed her sitting there, watching and observing. I asked her how she felt when she woke up and she said she felt lonely and awkward. She said she wondered where these places were and why no one was with her.

I said, 'People in our dreams represent our instincts and you listen to your instincts a lot. In real life, you've seen a lot of palaces – you live in one and you have visited lots of them around the world. However, I feel that the solitude in your dream represents a feeling you have in real life. Do you perhaps feel that your problems come from the rejecting attitude of others?'

She said that initially she had been looking forward to this particular royal visit, but that the dream had resurrected the sense of rejection she had experienced at the hands of palace officials when she was first married to Charles. She said she was tired of feeling isolated and wanted to be with her family in her dream. She asked herself in the dream, 'Why don't they come for me?'

I said, 'You are very, very, spiritual and you sense the problems of others acutely. It is time for you to try to tone down your sensitivity towards your family.' I then asked her, 'Did you see yourself as a silent witness in this?'

She nodded and said, 'Yes, but why couldn't I change this situation? I had been to the Queen and asked for her help with my feelings about travelling with Charles, and I told her of his constant phone calls to Camilla while we are away together. She was sympathetic but no one seemed to be able to improve the situation.'

Abandonment dreams

When people dream of being lost or abandoned in any way, it indicates that they are feeling alone and without the resources to help themselves. It is important to note that children experience being lost as being abandoned. To children, these two events are the same, giving rise to one and the same emotion. Such dreams are very disturbing as they heighten the childish fear of helplessness. Children who dream consistently along these lines may feel deserted by their parents. It is quite common for this sort of dream to occur at times of separation and divorce, when children feel that they are required to take sides or that somehow the failure of the marriage was their fault. It is very important for parents to be attuned to the needs of children during these difficult passages in adult relationships. For adults, it may feel as if their entire world has been pulled out from under them and that nothing is sure or secure.

Q: I had a dream of lying back in an endless sea, paralysed by fear. I am floating but feel I will sink, although I cannot move to save myself. There is no land in sight, no airplane or ship to be seen. I feel totally abandoned and utterly alone. I wake in tears. This dream has happened twice in the last month. I am presently going through a divorce.

JAN, MELBOURNE, AUSTRALIA

A: Men and women who are undergoing the difficult process of divorce often experience exceedingly painful dreams of abandonment. You are right in the middle of this process, so it is not surprising that your dream is recurring and agonising. If you set yourself some new goals and try to put the experience behind you, it will get better. Remember that it is important to learn from every experience, even abandonment, because if we do not learn from the trauma of parting we will remain stuck and unable to embrace life with vitality. Our dreams can help light our way forward.

FEELING ATTACKED

Diana's sense of insecurity as an adolescent expressed itself in other dreams. In one, she was being attacked or chased by an animal; in another, she was running over small islands of sand, and each one disintegrated as she stood on it. She felt as though she was being pursued by a large animal, and that it was about to catch her.

I said, 'I had dreams like that when I was growing up.'

She smiled and said, 'Thank goodness for that! I am dreaming like everyone else does! But what do they mean?'

'They are insecurity dreams,' I answered. 'As we feel the sand disappearing beneath us, we also feel as though we will fall away forever. These dreams generally appear when we are approaching our teenage years, a time when we don't really know who we are or who we will become. The fearsome animal chasing after us can symbolise all the concerns of the adult world we see before us.'

Diana went on to tell me a dream where she was being attacked by a dog. She was lying on green grass and looking up at the blue sky, and the dog, large and black, appeared and flew at her, snarling. He tore her clothes and she was so upset she began to cry – she was terrified and felt threatened.

I told Diana that most attack dreams indicate a sense of threat from someone close. Dogs traditionally act as guardians and so in symbolic terms tend to represent male figures. I asked her which male in her life might be threatening her. 'This could have been a non-sexual threat or a sexual one depending on what was happening to you at the time of this dream,' I said.

She said she had had this dream on her honeymoon and had woken up crying and calling out to Charles.

'Dogs represent loyalty and faithfulness too,' I said. 'Dreams of dogs can be very positive. Maybe you were feeling totally inexperienced sexually and this dream was, in its positive sense, a reminder to stop feeling under threat and remind yourself that you were a safely married woman and that your husband was not there to threaten you but to love you. I would say it was a "wake up to yourself" dream, telling you that you could no longer hide your fears of your sexuality from your subconscious or from your husband.'

In retrospect, it occurred to me that, during

her honeymoon, Diana might have been trying very hard to turn her husband's thoughts and desires towards her. I suspect she was already feeling the threat, subliminally, of his long-standing relationship with Camilla.

Aggressive animals in dreams

Animals in our dreams symbolise a wide range of emotional states. Frightening animals point to a discrepancy between our rational state and our deepest instincts. If they are chasing or threatening us in dreams, then it usually signifies that our instincts have been distorted in real life – wounded feelings or rage have been suppressed, for example. Animals can also make very positive appearances in our dreams, as the following dream shows.

Q: In my dream, I heard a noise, so I walked out my back door and I saw hundreds of dogs. They were all walking quietly about and I didn't feel frightened at all. Suddenly, in the middle of them was a very large dog. He was the most beautiful thing with a magnificent long coat that was so white it almost shone. The dog stood very still and looked at me and I had a feeling of such peace. I always remember my dreams by the 'feel' of them.

RICHARD, BRISBANE

A: Dogs in our dreams are our guardians. Your dog was obviously the leader of the pack. Your white shining dog is an indicator of excellent prospects in whatever you are undertaking.

Q: For the past 20 years I have been having a recurring dream about cats. These cats are often lions, tigers, panthers, cheetahs, etc. In my dream, they are always attacking me and, just as I am about to be killed, I wake up in a terrible sweat. What does this mean?

JENNY, CORNWALL

A: Your subconscious decided to pick the premier cats of this world for your dream images. The domestic cat depicts our comfort zone. When we have the cat on our lap, we stroke and fondle it in an enjoyable fashion but I wouldn't want to start doing that to the cats in your dream! You picked the untamed cats of this world so I tend to think that you have the same traits in your personality. Ask yourself – are there vital parts of me that are struggling to be made known?

FALLING FROM GRACE

Diana undoubtedly had high ideals and aspirations for herself in her everyday life. She told me that she frequently dreamt about falling from a high building. I told her that falling (from a cliff or from a very high building, or in a lift, for example) represents the dreamer's fears that their ambitions may be beyond their abilities. Or they may fear falling down in the eyes of someone. Falling down in one's own estimation in a dream suggests insecurity.

When Diana first talked to me about her falling dreams, I asked her, 'What is going on? Are you being pressured about something that is too big to mention? Does falling in your dreams relate to your past, do you think?'

We talked about it for a while and, when I pressed her to tell me what was happening in her everyday life at the time of the dreams, the penny dropped. She said, 'When I think of why I am having these falling dreams, I realise that on the day of the dream I always have meetings with the palace gurus and the Queen. Not always on the same day but around the time of when the dreams bother me.'

Then I asked her about other features of the dream. The colour purple stood out in her mind. I said, 'Then the message here is for you to please take note of this dream. Colour is there to help you recall what happened. In dream symbolism, an outstanding colour stands for awareness.' Then I thought for a moment. 'The interesting thing about the colour purple is that it is traditionally associated with royalty. So it seems that you are feeling very insecure about these meetings with your royal relatives.'

Another important feature of the dream was the ending. She never hit the ground in her fall. She would swoop up at the last minute. However, the anxiety she felt while falling would always wake her. I felt that this was a good sign – she was not being crushed by the fall, and there was a definite end to the scenario which was positive. I told her that I felt that she could overcome her insecurities with the royals and that her dream was telling her this.

Falling in dreams

Falling symbolises fear of failure or loss of power or control – for example, 'falling in love'. Falling may indicate an overweening ambition, or suggest that the dreamer is living too much in the intellect and neglecting more basic aspects of their physical and emotional wellbeing. Superstition has it that we will die if we hit the ground in a falling dream, but there is nothing to indicate that this is true. Often, the ground or water transforms itself on impact in a dream of this nature. If you are falling somewhere that is familiar to you, such as from a balcony in your house or from a ladder that you own, when you are awake, go and check the site. Our subconscious often picks up on details that we miss in our conscious state.

Your dream may be your subconscious's way of warning you of danger.

Q: I often dream about a cliff and rocks. Someone gets killed because he falls during a rock-climbing lesson. The police put a tape around the area. Then lots of kids appear around the edge of the taped area. The police try to disperse them but the kids run down to the edge of the cliff and start fighting. I sit there unable to move, watching the whole thing. I'm very scared.

JERRY, HOLBORN

A: Observing others who might fall suggests that you are under the influence of your peer group and you have some big decisions to make, whether to be strong and go it alone, or go with them! Make a decision and then your dream will go away.

DROWNING IN EMOTION

Diana was a strong swimmer and loved the water – so she was especially upset when she began having dreams about frightening tidal waves. In one such dream, she was alone behind tall glass doors that looked out on to the ocean from a huge house on a cliff. She saw an enormous wave approaching. As it crashed into the glass doors, she felt herself scream. No sooner had this wave dissipated than the next one came. She woke up as one of the waves smashed through the glass in the dream. She was absolutely transfixed and unable to move and had broken out in a cold sweat.

I told Diana that it was understandable for her to dream this way – she had to hold back her emotions and feelings about so many people and things. She was worried about what the dream might mean as far as her love of swimming was concerned. I described to her what water meant to us symbolically in dreams.

'Water symbolises our emotions. If it is clear, calm water then this means we feel peaceful in our real life, whereas if it is dirty or muddied then there is something "below the surface", so to speak. If there are waves and a feeling of fear, then this is associated with a build-up of emotional stress. This dream has nothing to do with your swimming. It was expressing how "built up" your emotions were at the time – and had been building up for a very long time, I imagine.'

I went on: 'One of the more unpleasant water dreams people have involves the toilet. This can be a rather repellent image for the dreamer.'

Diana replied, 'No, really! How disgusting! I would hate to dream like that! You're joking?'

I said, 'No, I'm not – some people have extremely unpleasant dreams about themselves and toilets. The meaning is usually simple. In their everyday lives, they find it impossible to release their emotions and thus the image of release appears in their dreams to help them identify the problem. The symbol behind water is an important one. No matter how water appears in our dreams, the message from our subconscious is to take immediate notice and try to fix the emotional problem that it describes.'

My explanation of the tidal-wave dream made sense to Diana. She said she had to hide her real feelings from so many people and sometimes felt like a sort of Jekyll and Hyde character. I said, 'Emotional stress in daily life takes its toll and your dreams are alerting you to that.'

Water in dreams

Water is a common feature in dreams – it may be threatening, mysterious, dangerous or have sexual overtones. There are many meanings, but water usually signifies the emotional wellbeing of the dreamer. A running river suggests the stream of emotional life. Is the water in this river turbulent, or free-flowing and gentle? The state of the water will alert you to the emotional state that is being highlighted. Calm water is usually pleasant to dream about, suggesting inner resources that we can draw on. If you are drowning in a dream, you may be feeling emotionally overwhelmed. Seeing a child drown in your dreams can represent an overprotective parent.

Q: The other night I dreamt so clearly that my two children and myself were bathing at the sea edge. Looking up, I saw a tall house by the shore. I was so entranced by the house that I called the children out of the water to look at it. As we approached, an enormous wave washed right over us and started to draw the house into the sea! Panicking, I urged my children up the sand towards the land. I grabbed two shoes, one belonging to me and one belonging to my daughter. The waves continued to wash over us, and the sand and sea swept the house away. I felt frantic. I could see my son crouched on a step, safe, but I couldn't see my daughter. The sand had washed over her, and suddenly I saw her to the right of the step where my son was. At this stage, I seemed to deliberately make myself wake up. Please analyse this dream for me, as it was so vivid and clear.

JEANETTE, DUBLIN, IRELAND

A: The ocean in your dream depicts significant emotions that have built up. In fact, they have become so pent up that your subconscious is showing you a picture of a catastrophic letting go. The

72

house is the symbol of self and you seemed to be entranced by it. This feeling, coupled with the water, points to a period in your life of intense personal decision-making. Combined with the sand, the water represents a force for change: the sea represents how you feel within and the sand tells you that it is time for a change. The high-set house, seemingly on a cliff, and three of you on the sea edge, symbolise that you are on the edge of your own futures. There is also a strong implicit message that you need to protect yourself and your children from something or someone threatening you. Your insecurity is strongest in regard to your daughter. You seem to identify her with yourself, as indicated by the shoes you pick up.

Q: I am always dreaming of toilets. Looking for a toilet, finding a toilet and going to the toilet. There are usually no doors on these toilets. I don't mind this sort of dream while I am dreaming it, but I'm quite troubled by it when I think about it after I wake up. It's embarrassing!

MARYANNE, BIRMINGHAM

A: The toilets are symbolic. What is of most concern is that you are dreaming so frequently about them. This would indicate that you are not acting on the messages from your unconscious. You need to put your emotions and relationships in order because the toilet is a symbol of releasing and getting rid of your emotions instead of harbouring them. The condition of the toilets is associated with your emotions, too. If the toilets are clean then your emotions are clear and easy to manage, but if they are dirty, even filthy — as some report — then you have a very troubled emotional life. As the doors were open, you may also feel ashamed of your emotions in some way.

BURGEONING SEXUALITY

Diana remembered a vivid dream just before she was married. In the dream, she was

74

surrounded by snakes. The setting of the dream was an old farmhouse that she didn't recognise. She walked through the house looking for her father, hoping he would calm the anxiety she was feeling.

There were snakes everywhere: on the hallway floor; in the kitchen sink; under the beds; even outside the kitchen, hanging from flower baskets. The snakes were in sinuous clusters, groups of six or seven entwined together. 'Dreadful!' she said (Diana loved the word 'dreadful' and repeated it often to great effect).

She turned around in the dream and, as she did so, saw a snake by her foot. It bit her. She tried to scream but was so terrified that no sound came.

Diana was a virgin when she married and I wasn't surprised to hear of this snake dream.

'Snakes represent our sexuality and our life force. They are very strong dream symbols. Perhaps you were a bit fearful of your forthcoming marriage – apart from anything else, my understanding is that you were quite inexperienced sexually,' I suggested as delicately as I could. 'In this dream, you seem to be looking for your father as a sort of saviour figure. This, too, would be indicative of a virginal young woman about to be married. The father figure is your strongest protector. But, on the way, you are bitten by the snake. I suggest this symbolises the forthcoming nuptials about which you felt excitement but also a sort of dread. Does this sound correct?' I asked.

'Yes, that makes sense,' she replied.

'I think the sense of danger you felt concerned the sexual act. Many young girls dream this way when they have not experienced sexual intercourse,' I said. 'Basically, the snake represents the penis and its venom, semen. There is no doubt that snake dreams are often related to the sexual thoughts and feelings of the dreamer.'

Diana was always curious about symbols in dreams and this snake symbolism fascinated her. I told Diana that powerful or frightening animals in dreams, such as bulls and stallions – animals known for their virility – could also be interpreted this way.

When she was having these dreams Diana

was still very dependent upon her father; but she was also looking forward to her role as wife of the future King of England. Diana said many times that she idealised marriage as a fantasy. She said to me that day, 'I had so many wonderful fantasies as a young girl. I wanted and hoped that my husband would look after me. He would take over the father-figure role and he would support and encourage me. I always thought my marriage would be forever, not end in divorce like my parents.' I thought I would be protected by the royal family. But it didn't happen, did it?'

I reassured her that many girls had the same experience as she did and that they had the same hopes and dreams for their future. 'Unfortunately, life is often not as we expect it to be. We must grow from – and through – the sad and bitter experiences.'

We ended this session talking and laughing a little about another dream she'd had since the snake dream. 'Maybe Charles will never be king,' she said, 'because I had a dream about him trying on a crown, but it kept falling off!'

Snake dreams

The snake can both kill and cure. It is also associated with renewal due to the fact that it loses and replaces its skin. The snake in many cultures represents the source of life, often the masculine source. The snake is broadly symbolic of our deepest and most potent creative power.

Q: In my first dream, I saw a long python in a tree in our back yard. Then I dreamt that I saw the same python in the same tree but it was moving towards the house. I closed the fly-wire screen door where my father was standing and asked him why he didn't shut the door, in case the python got into our house. Then I shut the door myself. The snake came up to the door handle and was going to bite it but my father just stood there, staring.

ANNABEL, DARWIN, AUSTRALIA

A: In your dream, your father represents your beginnings and the python signifies your sexuality. You live in Darwin, a place where snakes are part of the scenery, so you know both their power and their danger. The fact that your dream snake was ready to strike means you are feeling worried about the next stage of your maturity that is fast approaching. Your father will no longer be able to 'protect' you – you will need to find your own inner power and creative sources. But, remember, snakes are associated with free-flowing energy and wisdom. Time for you to take on their positive points, as well as being wary.

Q: I have dreams about lots of snakes in the filing cabinet at work. When I try to pull them out and cut them in half to kill them, they keep coming back!

JOE, MANCHESTER

A: Remember the saying 'snake in the grass'? For you, it is snakes in the filing cabinet. Watch out for some slimy and poisonous traits in your work group. You tried your best to handle the snakes in your dream – which shows your power and strength – but they 'resurrect' themselves and come back. Do you find at work that your ideas are not always listened to because you don't have enough support from colleagues? Take inspirations from the snakes and keep coming back, even though it may be tough. Watch your back and look for allies.

SELF-IMAGE

Diana told me that she had some dreams about her teeth falling out around the time of her engagement. 'It was a horrible dream,' she said. 'I didn't like it. I was so relieved when I woke up and found that my teeth were all still in place!'

I replied, 'People have that dream all over the world. The details vary from person to person but usually it includes the sensation of catching your teeth as they fall out of your mouth. Did you catch your teeth?'

'Yes, and it wasn't very pleasant at all,' she said.

'Our teeth signify our independent self-image, our communication and our nourishment. When teeth fall out in a dream, the image may be connected to a deflated self-image or a fear of old age or impotence (not in your case though). These dreams can also alert us to insufficiencies in our diet. Actors and actresses experience this dream quite often and it's thought that it relates to them having to change identity so often – and also that this identity is so often expressed through different ways of speaking and different accents.

'In your case, I would say that it's to do with your sudden visibility in the eyes of the world – you would have been feeling very aware of your image and how you appeared to those around you who were scrutinising your every move. It could have represented your concerns about your lack of communication skills at that time, and perhaps an unconscious fear of ageing, too.'

Teeth falling out dreams

To lose your teeth in dreams is to feel exposed and defenceless. It indicates a loss of confidence or power in a fundamental sense, or an inability to find a strong sense of identity in a current situation. This image is quite common in dreams but it is still a disconcerting experience. The mouth is our first point of nourishment and it depicts our self-image, both visually and verbally. Ask yourself if you have a tendency to use bad language. Are you often at a loss for words? Older parents can lose their teeth in their dreams due to their increasing age and diminished responsibilities in regard to their children. Is someone or something in your life causing you to suffer from a diminished self-image? Perhaps you are emotionally threatened at work or at home and are feeling inhibited. The dreamer who suffers frequently from this dream should also consider a visit to the dentist.

Q: I dreamt that I looked in the mirror to examine my teeth and they seemed to be growing bigger and overcrowding my mouth. I kept trying to push them back in, as they wouldn't stay in place. There was blood on my gums and my mouth wouldn't shut properly, but no teeth actually fell out.

SHERIE, TASMANIA, AUSTRALIA

A: Looking in the mirror and seeing your overcrowded mouth full of teeth suggests that you could be facing an identity crisis. Teeth in dreams often point to a fear of getting old and a loss of image, but as there was blood it could be that what you were concerned about is over and finished. The dream does reflect an anxiety associated with either the original loss of baby teeth or neglect on the part of the dreamer to care for their teeth. An inadequate diet and use of bad speech or language is also connected with a dental dream.

CHAPTER 4

ALONE ON THE STAGE

'Dreams are a spontaneous self-portrayal,
in symbolic form, of the actual situation
in the unconscious.'

CARL GUSTAV JUNG

OVER time, Diana became adept at turning a
double negative into a triple positive! She knew
she had to encourage her independence to
survive – and she did. From the start of her
marriage, she knew that she was being
'overlooked' but she continued to try to please
her husband.

The 'People's Princess' established her sense
of identity through fashion – she felt that
her clothes were her chief channel of
communication with the public. Dubbed
'Dynasty Di' by the media in 1987 for her love

of glamorous gowns, she adopted ever-more provocative outfits in order to gain her husband's attention. By the time I met her in 1996, she had accepted that her life with Charles was long over. She sold her collection of dresses and took control of her life.

DANCE THE BLUES AWAY

Diana loved to dance. She told me she would have loved to have been a ballet dancer – even though she knew she was too tall. She always enjoyed official engagements more if there was dancing, preferably in a ballroom, and she reminisced to me how thrilling had been one of her first-ever dances with Charles.

When she told me that she had recently dreamt she was a ballerina, I told her, 'This shows you that you can be whatever you want to be, even if it's only in your dreams. To dance in dreams is to rise above yourself and your cares. It can symbolise an urge to escape from the material world and signifies a lightness of spirit.'

She replied that the dream had been quite sensual and enjoyable.

Diana then told me about a dancing dream that was less pleasant. For Prince Charles's birthday in 1985, Diana decided to give him a surprise. She had spent the weeks in the run-up to Charles's birthday rehearsing a routine with Royal Ballet dancer Wayne Sleep.

On the night of Charles's birthday, he and Diana were at the Royal Opera House, watching a benefit performance for the Friends of Covent Garden. Halfway through, Diana slipped out of the Royal Box, got changed and suddenly appeared on stage, where she danced in front of Charles to the strains of Billy Joel's 'Uptown Girl'.

Diana told me how nervous she had been before her performance. She had dreamt that she was watching a figure on stage wrapped in a long cloak. The figure was shuffling around on the stage like some old, shambolic drunk and in her dream Diana felt worried and troubled by what she was seeing. She had this dream several times.

I said, 'I think the shuffling figure you were so worried about is yourself. Even though you were practising hard and wanted to be perfect for Charles, you were still worried that you would somehow fail. You decided to see the figure – yourself – as a shuffling nobody instead of who you really were, one of the most famous people in the world. But you did dance on that stage. You conquered the fear within you.'

Dancing dreams

Dancing symbolises physical energy being directed from chaos to order and transformed to mean something at a higher level. It is one of the most ancient forms of magic. It has been said that dancing dreams are tunes from the heart. The dance in dreams often has an erotic energy, but most importantly it identifies the dancer with liberation and some sort of inner union between body and soul. If the dream dance or dancer is clumsy or inept, then the dance points to a breakdown in that union.

Q: I dreamt I was in a room dancing close to a dark-haired guy – he was teaching me 'dirty dancing', like in the movie of that name. The next thing I knew we were in a place that had lots of rooms but no doors. We walked into a room and some of his friends were sitting on the floor, so he joined them. I was about to do the same when music began to play, so I grabbed a pillow and started to practise the dance he taught me. He – the guy – saw what I was doing and he got up and danced with me. When he did, his friends disappeared. Then I woke up. In the dream, I felt that I loved him even though he did not show any affection towards me. It was just the fabulous dancing!

JULIET, LIVERPOOL

A: I think you need to get out and dance! This dream depicts the pure pleasure to be had from moving your body in a free-flowing way. You do not say whether you have a boyfriend in real life, but if you don't I think it's time you sought one out. The fact that his friends disappeared when you both started to dance suggests that friendships are not what you are subconsciously seeking – you need to feel an erotic charge in your life as well.

IN HER OWN IMAGE

During my second visit to the palace, Diana remarked on my Chanel boots, which had CC's intertwined in a badge on the front. She said to me, 'Well, Joan, I am glad to see that you have worn your Charles and Camilla's!'

I laughed. 'What about your shoes?' I asked.

'These are my tart shoes,' she replied. They were high-heeled Christian Dior slingbacks. 'They are my Charles and Diana's!' she said, laughing. She then told me that she often dreamt about shoes, and asked me what that meant.

'Were they women's shoes?' I asked.

'Yes,' she said, 'and there were so many of them. They were all lined up in twos and they were in a huge department-store window.'

'Were they coloured shoes or just black?'

'They were all different colours and there were two pairs that attracted me the most, but they were odd, the colours didn't match. I can't remember the colours.'

I then asked, 'What do shoes mean to you?'

'I love them,' she said. 'I have oodles of pairs of shoes!'

'Just like Imelda Marcos?' I asked.

'No, not as many as her,' she said, giggling.

'Well, it must have felt frustrating in your dream if you couldn't get the shoes you wanted?' I suggested.

'Yes, it was, and I was getting quite annoyed.'

I thought about this. 'Shoes in dreams symbolise our external image. You, more than most people, must always be conscious of how you appear to the outside world. Shoes appearing in your dreams reflects this. The shoes in the shop were somehow not available to you and this could indicate that you were not taking opportunities that surrounded you at the time of your dream.

'Shoes are also very feminine dream symbols and are related to sexuality. Hats and gloves are the same. You are a fashion icon, so let's face it: you always get the shoes you want! But, in your dream, the shoes you liked were not paired up properly. Dreaming of things in pairs signifies a matching up, a balancing of male and female. In your case, the pairs didn't match.'

After this analysis, I also offered a little practical advice: 'Always try to remember what happened on the day of a dream. This helps sort out the subliminal messages from the subconscious messages. You may have been out shopping for shoes on the day of your dream and this dream was just a "pick up" on events that happened that day.'

Clothing and shoes in dreams

Clothing in dreams, if very colourful, can represent the positive aspects of the dreamer's psychological or spiritual growth. But if the clothes are overly elaborate this may suggest a weakness or a pretension in the dreamer. Clothes can make you look completely different – for example, thinner, taller, richer or poorer – and can therefore signify wish-fulfilment or even indicate hypocrisy. An amazing technicoloured coat in a dream could stand for the dreamer trying to deceive others. An old superstition often reported is that for a young girl to dream of putting on new clothes means she will marry soon. Dreams where shoes, purses, handbags or gloves feature prominently usually relate to some sexual aspect of the dreamer. These items of clothing depict female genitalia. Women's shoes are sometimes associated with a dominant sexuality on the part of the dreamer – but if the shoe or shoes are uncomfortable, then there is something in the dreamer's life that just does not 'fit'.

Q: My dream took place in a location like something out of a Western movie. I was a cowboy's girlfriend – even though I hadn't even watched a Western in years. My boyfriend had been captured by an outlaw, who was after me as well. He tracked me down to an old, dilapidated house where we had a shoot-out. He eventually got into the house and captured me. He told me he was going to hang me and my boyfriend and began to wrap clothing – shirts, shorts and jeans – around our ankles. As he wrapped the clothes around, they fell off, but he kept going, wrapping and letting them fall off. Eventually, he wrapped some sheets around our waists and told us he was going to hang us like that from a window. The clothes seemed to be a really important aspect of the dream: in one part, I was laden down with many layers of drab, tattered garments which I had to laboriously peel off, one by one.

TERRY, SYDNEY, AUSTRALIA

A: To dream of being tied up indicates your need for freedom. It certainly was a colourful experience in every way: colour in dreams is there to ensure we remember what happens after we wake. I think you are in need of a change. There seems to be a transition theme running through your images. You describe how the outlaw ties on clothes and how they keep falling off, and how you are covered in layers and layers of clothing that you must take off 'laboriously'. This indicates that whatever transition you are going through will be long and difficult, but that you will move on with your life – whether it is with or without those around you now. Try to treat your future as an adventure like your dream.

THE PRINCESS AT LARGE

Another dream Diana told me about was where she was wearing her most 'princess-like' accessories – her tiara and jewels. She was outside a huge domed building and a long red carpet stretched before her. As she walked along the carpet towards the building, she felt a mounting sense of excitement. She then entered a magnificent room. In its centre was a huge U-shaped table where she was to be seated.

'Did you recognise anyone?' I asked.

'No,' she replied, 'it just seemed like another one of those familiar formal occasions I always went to. Then, suddenly, waiters and waitresses appeared. They were carrying dishes and they began flinging them like frisbees! They seemed to be playing some sort of game.'

Then this scene changed. Everyone was seated and eating their meals – except Diana, who had been given nothing to eat. She felt extremely sad, and realised that the only time she had been really happy in the dream was when she was watching the waiters and waitresses throwing the plates.

We discussed events surrounding her at the

time. She had been feeling bitterly disappointed because she had not been invited to attend a reception that the Queen had given for Nelson Mandela, despite the fact that the royal family knew Mandela was one of Diana's heroes. She was separated from Prince Charles; she was experiencing loneliness and isolation and she was more than a little anxious about her future role.

I told her I felt that her dream symbolised her feelings of acute disappointment at not being part of the reception for Mandela, which she would have regarded as tremendous fun – hence the flying plates. The dream also seemed to relate to her more generalised feelings of isolation from the royal family, even though she was still expected to be one of them. Diana had also come to relish big events such as this. They gave her chance to meet interesting and powerful people and made her life more exciting. Now she was anxious that it was all slipping away – just at the point where she had evolved from the shy teenager who had married Prince Charles into a mature and confident woman.

I noticed after we spoke about this dream that Diana went to great lengths to appear even more magnificent than usual at public events and functions. Especially now that she was attending them alone.

Dreams of famous people

If you dream of being friends with famous people, it indicates that you need to be less intimidated by those around you. Mixing with royalty or celebrities in dreams tends to make the dreamer realise their worth and raises their self-esteem: 'If I can make it with them, I can make it with anyone.' Celebrity dreams add colour and significance to what the dreamer may see as their dull existence. Dreamers will often enjoy sexual encounters with the 'stars' of their dreams. In this case, the illustrious dream partner usually holds a conscious significance for the dreamer. It may be that they embody characteristics the dreamer finds especially attractive, erotic or just downright sexy. We are confronted daily with delicious beings who strut their stuff through our various media. It's impossible not to notice them. There's not much point in worrying too much about a pleasurable dream of this nature. Just lie back and enjoy – after all, it's most unlikely that the dream star will affect your real life. Once again, the dream may simply point to areas that are lacking in your own life. It simply may be that you are looking for a little extra excitement.

Q: In my dream, I am good friends with Madonna, though none of my friends will believe me. I specifically remember asking her if I should cut my hair short or grow it long, and then asking if she will give me a video-tape of her film *In Bed With Madonna*. When she leaves, we hug and kiss goodbye behind some rocks. Will I become friends with Madonna in real life?

SANDY, BALLAN, AUSTRALIA

A: Probably not! Knowing famous people is a great boost for your ego. If we dream of ourselves enjoying their company, it heightens our self-esteem. The feeling is rather along the lines of 'If I can mix with Madonna, I can mix with anyone'. Perhaps you need to be more ambitious socially.

Q: The Queen asked me to have afternoon tea with her at Buckingham Palace. She served me and we sat together – she even knew my name. Prince Philip came into the room and she introduced me to him. As I stood up, I dropped my scones and felt uneasy. The Queen smiled and then I was fine again. I could describe the entire scene after my dream.

MARY, SHEFFIELD

A: Seeing the Queen so comfortable and relaxed – and remembering the scene so vividly afterwards – indicates that your everyday life may have become a tad ordinary. After this dream, you feel you are on cloud nine, because if you can dine with the Queen then you are 'up there' with the best of them.

PAPARAZZI DARLING

The paparazzi were an almost constant feature in Diana's life from the moment her relationship with Prince Charles was made public until her untimely death.

At first, she had no idea how to handle the unremitting attention. As crowds of photographers pursued her from her kindergarten, she would race, head down and blushing furiously, for her little red mini. The press loved it and Diana soon learned to play on her shyness to win them over even more. She captured the hearts of the media forever when, naively, she agreed to pose for photographers outside her kindergarten. With the sunlight behind her, the resultant photograph seemed to show Diana wearing a see-through skirt. A star was born!

When I met Diana, she was no longer the innocent young woman portrayed in those photographs and news images. She was a beautiful princess – and a skilled, media-savvy operator. For those who once characterised Diana as none-too-bright, this was no mean feat. In her dealings with the media, she rarely put a foot wrong. This required a steely determination and constant vigilance. She had worked out exactly what the world's press needed, and gave it to them in carefully rationed doses.

So I wasn't at all surprised that one of Diana's dreams related specifically to the media.

We were sitting on the comfortable green sofa in Kensington Palace and Diana was talking about the paparazzi and how she hid from them initially. She went on to tell me some of her many, many experiences with them. I loved these conversations with her because she laughed a lot and talked with her hands. Her run-ins with the paparazzi had certainly left their mark on her.

She described her dream as taking place somewhere that was dark and 'mulchy'. It was protected by a huge gate. 'I didn't know the place,' she said. 'I felt it was dangerous to be there. When I looked up at the gate, which had no handle, there were hundreds of eyes looking through little holes in the gate. I was worried and wondered what they were looking at. I looked up at the black sky that was shining with stars and began to feel more comfortable.

Then I seemed to be gliding towards the gate. I didn't want to, but I felt I had to be brave and find out more about the eyes that were looking at me: were they people's eyes? Or animal eyes? It felt so mysterious. It was only when I got up close that I could see that they were not staring at me but blinking – blinking and blinking incessantly. The thought came into my head, "Not them again!" The eyes felt like insects, mosquitoes crawling all over me. As I came up close to the gate, I felt as though my feet were sinking into the mulch. I looked up at the sky again and the stars seemed to be dancing. At that moment, I woke up and I felt fabulous! But how could I, after such a mysterious dream? Do you think those eyes were the paparazzi cameras that are always focused on me and never on Charles?'

I replied, 'Your dream about eyes and stars was wonderful. Let me say that eyes in our dreams give us clues to our spiritual health and, as the saying goes, are regarded as windows to the soul. As you are the dreamer, it is you who "sets" the tone and feeling of the images in your dream, so if you feel that the eyes were cameras then that's what they probably were. Perhaps you felt that the photographers wanted to capture your soul. Maybe they could have at one stage of your life, but not now.'

I continued, 'The stars were a magical image in your dream. Rarely is this image regarded as negative, so I think that the gate – which symbolises an opening to a new world of enlightenment – and the stars, which are connected to fate, combine to make this dream a story of your inner journey and how you have conquered the outside influences on your life. This dream tells me that you are in control.'

Diana rolled her eyes, as if to say, 'At last!'

Dreaming of stars

We look to the stars in the hope of working out our destiny. It is no surprise that Diana, one of the 'stars' of her generation and the most photographed woman of her time, made the connection between photographers and stars, as well as eyes watching her. If we dream of stars, it may mean that we are yearning for a stronger spiritual significance in our lives, and the desire to tap mysterious powers that may help determine our fate.

Q: Last night I dreamt of being in the outback. It was hot and the sun was beaming down on me. Then, suddenly, I was in the dark. I looked up and saw lots of stars to my right. But there was one star, all on its own, away from the others. It was much brighter than the rest, too, and seemed so close to me – in fact, it looked as though it was heading towards me. I woke up at this point. I live in the countryside, where you can always see lots of stars at night anyway, but was there more to it than that?

ESTHER, ALICE SPRINGS, AUSTRALIA

A: While the sun represents your strong intellect and your emotional strength, the stars are connected to your life journey and your spirituality. The star that was close to you in your dream is your very own star – the one you should follow. Are you in the process of making some big decisions about your life? The star is telling you to trust in your intuition. The other stars, on your right side (the side of the brain associated with intuition and creativity) support this theme. Be encouraged and take the leap of faith that you know is right.

CHAPTER 5

CHARLES AND CAMILLA

'The imagination may be compared to Adam's dream – he awoke and found it truth.'
JOHN KEATS

FOR Prince Charles, marriage was a matter of duty. He even used former and current lovers, most notably Camilla, to help him find a suitable wife. Moving in high circles, they were ideal researchers in Charles's quest for marriage material. His adored great-uncle Lord Mountbatten even chipped in with some sage advice: 'A man should sow his wild oats and have as many affairs as possible before settling. But for a wife he should choose a suitable and sweet-hearted girl before she meets anyone else she might fall for.'

In August 1980, at the annual party for

Cowes Week, Charles confided to a friend that he had found the girl he was going to marry – Lady Diana Spencer. In February 1981, Charles proposed to Diana and she accepted. But throughout their courtship Charles continued to see his long-time lover, Camilla Parker Bowles. A couple of weeks before the wedding, Diana opened a parcel in her office and to her surprise saw that it was a gold bracelet with an enamel disc bearing two Cs, signifying Charles and Camilla's secret intimacy. It had been ordered by Charles as a gift for Camilla. Charles and Diana's marriage was always to have a secret third party whom Diana, naturally, resented.

OFF WITH HIS HEAD!
Diana described a dream she had just before she steeled herself to see the Queen, to ask her what to do about the relationship between Charles and Camilla.

In her dream, she was in her office in Kensington Palace and around her she saw a wall of filing cabinets. She started opening them and closing them and her frustration at what she was trying to find was making her extremely anxious.

She said, 'I had in my hand what I considered to be a very important document and yet I couldn't read the words. I felt myself getting angry because I knew I couldn't find whatever I was looking for in the cabinets and I still had this sheet of paper in my hand. I looked down as I moved through the office and the piece of paper burst into flames. It didn't burn me and I just kept pulling out the drawers, trying to discover the file or what it was that I must find. Then, I opened one of the drawers and there, to my horror, was the decapitated head of Charles. It was just sitting there, looking at me. I wasn't afraid, though. I just thought, "Well, what will the Queen say when I tell her?" Why wasn't I afraid? It wasn't a nice dream, after all.'

I replied, 'Finding a decapitated head of someone that you care for in dreams is not what you think. It may look horrific, but our dreams love to dramatise our anxieties. Seeing Charles this way occurred because you were having arguments and misunderstandings – to say the least – at this time. The beheading of

Charles indicates your need to rid yourself of your problems and to make him less powerful in your life. When the paper burst into flames, this symbolised your anger and emotions that were becoming more and more bottled up and which had driven you to try to sort things out with the Queen. Our subconscious loves to shock us with our dream images.'

Shocking dream images

Shocking images in our dreams are simply strong symbols that frighten us into remembering, and hopefully doing something about, our dreams. It is very important to remember that most dreams are not literal. They work on a symbolic level. Images such as beheading or maiming, or even murder, usually point to a strong emotion that the dreamer feels about something that is happening in their everyday life.

Q: I recently had a dream that left me feeling quite shaken. My boyfriend and I were at a party. We were sitting at a table and as I got up to leave I saw an old woman. She was sitting in a rocking chair, rocking back and forth. Her eyes were blazing red and she had no arms and legs. I looked away in fear. Then I noticed my boyfriend get up from the table and head for the door. I screamed and screamed at him not to leave me with the frightening old woman, but he couldn't hear me. I was so scared that I jumped out of the window trying to stop him. Please tell me what this means.

CHRIS, QUEENSLAND, AUSTRALIA

A: You are living in fear of losing your boyfriend to old age and infirmity. The frightening old woman is you. But your dream shows you what you should be doing – leaping through the window of your emotions and acting to grab love and happiness. Jump as you did in your dream and you will float above all the obstacles that may be surrounding you and your love life. Your subconscious has shocked you into action.

RAPACIOUS BIRDS

Diana once experienced a vivid dream about birds that expressed her emotions about Charles and Camilla. Blackbirds everywhere, she said, like an Alfred Hitchcock movie!

'I was on a small sailboat and I looked up and these birds were all over the sail, and I think I could hear the sound of their wings flapping, or it may have been the water lapping against the boat. It was calm and peaceful in the dream, yet above me was this crazy scene of birds. It occurred to me in the dream, "Why weren't they seagulls?" I tried to stand up and the boat rocked and made it impossible and I wondered why, because the water was so calm. I woke up feeling that this dream was quite weird.'

I told her that birds in dreams often relate to our sense of freedom, but they can also symbolise certain aspects of our relationships. The fact that the birds were blackbirds and not seagulls – or doves, for that matter – was crucial to working out what it meant. We talked about blackbirds and what they represented in real life as well as what they represented to Diana particularly. They are territorial, noisy, not very attractive and often connected to fairy stories. Diana also thought they were unpleasant and quite common. I thought that they indicated a feeling Diana had that she didn't like or want to admit: I told Diana that the birds reflected her jealous thoughts.

She agreed that she had been incredibly jealous of Charles and Camilla's relationship. It was something she abhorred but had to live with.

I suggested that the boat on calm water was about another part of her life: she was able to sail smoothly through most things, her life was under control, but the blackbirds were pecking away at her equilibrium. The fact that she tried to stand up, and couldn't, also indicated to me that her jealousy – represented by the birds – was a powerful force in her life at the time.

I added that the sound of flapping was her subconscious's way of making her remember the dream.

'I know now that Charles will never give up that woman,' she said. When we talked further, it seemed to me that she was in the process of accepting this fact. The dream had been about Diana's struggle to come to terms with the situation – a struggle which I think she ultimately won.

Bird dreams

Flying birds represent freedom, escape and movement in another dimension – transcendence. In primitive society's tribal shamans, or holy men, don bird masks to 'fly' through the world. Birds are associated with the higher self and have spiritual connotations. Like angels, they indicate the soul, and the yearning for release from the physical plain. However, birds also have a negative side. Their sharp beaks can rip and shred and pierce, and their cries can be harsh and shrill. In this manifestation, they are not uplifting but rather represent a downward emotional spiral– the image shows the dreamer that darker impulses are impeding their spiritual transcendence.

Q: I am walking my basset hound in my dream and when we come to a tree I see two parrots, one a vivid blue and the other bright green. I think to myself, 'When we get near they will fly away,' but

114

I open my arms and one flies into them and the other picks up my dog's lead in her beak. A friend appears and I tell them that I have always wanted a parrot. I say that I will call one Emerald and the other Sapphire. I ask my friend to get me something to put the birds in and she produces a black bin bag. I wake up at this point. I told a friend about this dream and said that someone she knew had a parrot called Ruby. I didn't know this when I had the dream. Please help me work out what it all means.

SUE, LONDON

A: Are you a lady who loves jewellery? Have you been loitering near jewellery stores, wishing for something new and glamorous in your life? Well, it will happen because this is a very important dream. Your parrots were so colourful and your names for them were perfect. Colour in our dreams makes us remember – and parrots are by nature colourful creatures – so in this dream you are doubly reminding yourself to remember these jewel names. Jewels usually reflect major transformation in a positive way. Parrots are known also for their cleverness with words. The parrots are messengers that you are entering a phase of strong spiritual and personal happiness where you will find joy in self-expression.

HORSE-RIDING WITH CAMILLA

Diana once rang me from London to ask me about a horse-riding dream that she'd had. In the dream, she was riding a huge grey horse. She was sitting side-saddle and was confident and in control as she steered her mount along a track. 'The track,' she said, 'seemed to wind, then go straight, then wind again.'

As she went through the second series of bends, she saw a small horse – a Shetland pony – in the distance. A large person was sitting on it, and the pony was almost squashed as it tried gamely to trot along.

'I felt like trying to catch up with the pony and its mount,' she said, 'but I couldn't seem to move forward fast enough with my horse. I felt so frustrated because I had been riding brilliantly before I saw them.'

At first, she thought that the rider on the pony was a friend of hers, a riding companion from the days when she had taken horse-riding lessons from James Hewitt. As she slowly caught up to the small horse she could see that its rider was a woman – and one with a large *derrière*! 'It's Camilla!' she exclaimed to herself in her dream. The dream ended with Diana eventually overtaking the pony. When she did, Camilla would not look at her, pretending she had not noticed that Diana was there.

'Congratulations,' I said. 'This dream shows that you have come a long way. You were riding confidently – and side-saddle, to boot.'

Diana laughed. 'I spent much of my life scared of horses, having fallen from one when I was a child. It wasn't until James patiently taught me to ride that I conquered that dreadful fear.'

I then told her what horses mean symbolically in dreams. Horses are associated with our libido and free expression, our power, our strength and liveliness.

I told her that I found it interesting that she was riding so confidently, yet there were still traces of insecurity in her feelings of frustration. These feelings occurred when she couldn't catch up fast enough with the other rider – who, of course, turned out to be Camilla. The presence of the Other Woman restricted the positive power of the horse symbol.

Diana was silent for a moment and then she said, 'I tried hard to ride well, but I would much rather be skiing or swimming or dancing, I'm afraid. Give me a good gym workout, any time – especially over a horse ride with Camilla!'

Horse dreams

Horses in dreams can signify strength, clairvoyance, power, intense desires and instincts. They are signifiers of the state of our libido, in the broadest sense – the power of creative life within us. The colour of the horse tends to be quite important, with a white horse signifying life and spirit while a black horse depicts death. The horse can also be regarded as the mother within us: our intuitive, nurturing understanding of the world.

Q: In my dream I was standing on the front lawn with a beautiful white horse. There was a girl there and she told me the horse was dying. I ignored her and started to pat the horse. The horse was rubbing my back, then he fell down. He really was dying. I sat down next to the horse and kept patting him. The girl and I saw the horse die. I felt it was something very special.

KEITH, TASMANIA, AUSTRALIA

A: Your white horse, even though he was dying, represents a new stage of development for you, either in an energetic or intuitive sense. Your gentleness was evident in the dream and perhaps you love horses in everyday life. If so, you should still take the same message from this dream. I am sure that this dream was special, as you say, and I am also sure that you are surrounded by a strong, nurturing and creative force.

CHAPTER 6

THE ROYAL DIVORCE

'So may the outward shows be least themselves;
The world is still deceived with ornament.'

WILLIAM SHAKESPEARE,
THE MERCHANT OF VENICE

DIANA'S *Panorama* interview from November
1995 was seen by some as an act of self-
indulgence; I prefer to think of it as an act of self-
preservation. After exposing the truth of her life
on the BBC, she received thousands of letters
from women asking for help because they were
suffering from eating disorders, loneliness and
desperate unhappiness. They responded to
Diana's emotional openness that reflected their
own pain, sadness and isolation. On 28 August
1996, Diana became a single woman. Freed from
many of her royal duties – not to mention her

royal title – Diana was able to set about reinventing herself. She rose from the ashes of her marriage all the stronger. She was fit and healthy of body and mind. She wanted a new life.

FIGHT OR FLIGHT?

Diana was frightened by a dream where she was accompanied by a group of ladies dressed in black, and where her mouth was taped over. She was standing in front of what looked like an Ancient Greek temple. Behind it lay a giant sand dune with a stream of people walking along its crest in a perfect line. There were also footprints all over the sand around her. There were splashes of red everywhere. Diana felt it was paint rather than blood.

She said she felt threatened and frightened in the dream. I asked her how she had felt when she woke up. She told me she had been shaking and crying.

Diana had this dream when she should have been at her happiest, when she was with Dodi Fayed. This in itself frightened her. 'Why would I dream in this way when I'm feeling so wonderful?' she asked.

'Let's look at what happened on the day of the dream,' I said.

She said nothing abnormal had happened, other than the usual paparazzi following them everywhere.

I said, 'In the dream, you were in a foreign situation, unable to speak or to call out. I would guess that somewhere in your life you feel you are being controlled by forces stronger than yourself. The black – negative – figures surrounding you have strong threatening overtones. Being gagged depicts a need for freedom. Perhaps this message from your subconscious could also be associated with repressed sexual fantasies that you had as a child. The people in your dream could be your instincts and the historic building could mean that you have many acquaintances but few true friends: the building was totally impersonal to you, just a backdrop for your dream's imagery. Red symbolises passion, and colour is often present in our dreams as a message from the subconscious to ensure we take notice and remember the dream. The sand dune was interesting in that it is a symbol that often represents time. Is it time for you to make really big decisions?'

Diana was taken aback. She looked at me with complete seriousness. 'If only you knew,' she said.

Bondage dreams

Being tied up points to a sense of futility or helplessness in the dreamer – and the desire to escape a real-life situation. The dreamer may be apprehensive of life events that seem to offer them little choice. It may be that this sort of dream occurs when the dreamer's everyday life is held under tight control, either by themselves or someone else. Bondage has also been traditionally associated with sexual fetish, but this is not necessarily the case in the symbolic atmosphere of a dream.

Q: I don't have anything to do with animals in my life, so when I dreamt I was trying to set animals free from a zoo I was confused. I went about it so methodically, making sure that I had the tools with which to break open their cages. I was even wearing camouflage clothing and a balaclava, so that I wouldn't be seen or recognised. I really felt that I had to let the animals free: they were tied up in their cages, unable to move about, and I knew I had to release them. What can this mean?

ROB, WALES

A: You are trying to set yourself free – or, more specifically, your instincts and desires. It sounds as if you need to escape or be released from a vigorous psychological bondage. The dream is telling you in no uncertain terms to release your emotions in order to enjoy your hidden primal energies – and benefit from a real sense of libido in your life.

MAKING THE DECISION TO BREAK

I had a fabulous discussion with Diana just after her annual skiing holiday. She told me that during these trips she always slept really well and didn't suffer from any of the insomnia that often plagued her. She told me of dream she'd had while on holiday. It took place in a mountain cabin. 'I was making my way back to my cabin through the snow. It was set back apart from the other cabins around it in an isolated but very beautiful spot. Suddenly, a man appeared wielding a knife. I tried to run to the cabin, but he overtook me and ran into the cabin before me. When I got to the cabin, I didn't seem to be worried. I went in and began to look for him. I heard a sound in the basement and went down. The basement was filled with machines making armaments, like in a factory, and some guards were posted in front of a heavy-looking door. Then the door opened and Camilla was standing there. I ran back out into the snow – and then I woke up!'

'It was so dark in the basement, like a black hole,' she went on. 'I think the dream means that I should get away from Charles and leave him, even though I don't want to. Camilla is divorced so perhaps it means I should get divorced too. What do you think?'

I answered by asking Diana if she thought she had learned anything from the dream.

'Yes,' she answered, 'I think I should get out of the dark hole. I think the man with the knife was Charles. He didn't hurt me and I know that he would never harm me physically, not like he has hurt me emotionally, but he was there. It was very emotional seeing that man wielding a knife. I also felt the guards were there to observe, not protect, me.'

I told her, 'A dream can't take sides on what you should or shouldn't do. Dreams bring up certain factors and put them in stories to allow us to move forwards in life. It is important to remember that the dream doesn't make life decisions; the dreamer does.'

Weapons in dreams

The knife, dagger or sword is by far the most common male sexual symbol. It can represent the penis in its ability to penetrate, and can stand for masculinity in its associations with violence and aggression. It can also represent the 'sword of truth' that cuts through falsity and ignorance, or the will to cut away false desires. When wielded against the dreamer, it can also signify that he or she is feeling anxious about a significant loss of power. Arms in general represent the heavy, destructive power of war.

Q: I dreamt that I was going for a drive with my boyfriend and there was a strange lady that I didn't know with us. I was told to sit in the back seat while the lady sat in the front seat. My boyfriend was paying her a lot of attention and whenever I spoke to him it was as if he didn't even hear me. Then a man started chasing me with a knife and my boyfriend and the lady didn't notice.

HAYLEY, THE ISLE OF WIGHT

A: Being chased by someone with a knife symbolises your sexual needs are not being met by the one you love. You are taking a 'back seat' in your relationship. Instead of keeping silent or bursting out with some dramatic ultimatum, start making moves to really communicate your discontent to your current boyfriend or change partners.

BUILDING A NEW LIFE

When her divorce was going through, Diana began to experience dreams of decay and dilapidation. Each dream was slightly different but the themes were always the same. There would be an image of an enormous house, but the fence surrounding it would be in tatters. Instead of the lovely flowers Diana looked for in her dreams, she found only weeds. In another dream of the same type, the front of the house was very run down.

I told her that dreaming this way was very common and not to get too depressed about it. The house in her dream was herself and the fence in tatters meant that she was letting negative thoughts from outside invade her privacy and was not concentrating on her positive strengths. When she saw the front of the house in need of repair, this meant that she needed to keep herself looking glamorous because her ego was being undermined by her imminent divorce.

Many people dream of houses. The house in dream symbolism represents our physical body. A house that is run down and in need of repair can mean that your health is suffering. If your dream house is old and uncared for, then your physical strength is at a low ebb.

In Diana's house dream, she was in a tiny room and it was pitch black outside. There was very little light in the room, just enough to see the outline of the furniture. She was scared when she looked out of the small window into the dark.

Then the room slowly became colourful. There were people that she knew in the room. Somehow, she knew that there were four storeys in the house. Together with the other people, Diana went out of the small room and began to climb the stairs. As she did so, the stairs suddenly felt as though they would give way.

As she climbed the stairs, Diana saw at the top a man standing with his back to her. She couldn't see who it was, but knew it was someone she was attracted to. When Diana was almost at the top of the stairs the man turned around. It was her husband, Charles.

'Let's look at what the images mean,' I said. 'The dark room and window depict the disappearance of some vital aspects of your everyday life and of someone you love deeply. The colourful people represent, I think, your instincts, which are actually very sound and healthy. Climbing the stairs is a rhythmic action and, in Freudian symbolism, it is associated with our sexual self. As the stairs were unsafe, I would suggest that you are not fulfilling your sexual desires; they are, to say the least, shaky.'

'You could say that,' Diana said, holding up both of her hands to her face. I felt as though I had her full, undivided attention at this point. She had this dream right in the middle of her divorce from Charles and it was easy to see from the dilapidated house imagery that she was feeling threatened and insecure. I told her, 'Many people going through divorce have these types of dreams. The message from your subconscious in this case is to concentrate on your positive strengths and instincts. They will help to eliminate your negative energies.'

Dream houses

The house symbolises our physical body – our persona and how we operate actively in the world – so a house that is run down and in need of repair can mean your whole sense of self needs an overhaul. It can also indicate that your health is suffering. If you are young and this type of dream occurs, have a medical check-up. If you are old, and your dream house is old and uncared for, then your physical strength is at a low ebb.

Q: Over a decade or so, I've had dreams where I'm living in rundown houses that are just about habitable. They tend to be open to the elements and it is often the case that they suffer some sort of weather-related damage when there is no one home. In the most recent dream, I was living in a house on a high, sloping hill. It was a very windy day, and the house began to lift up. I was in the house at the time, and was lifted up, too. With the help of some friends I managed to keep the house from flying away – but all the walls collapsed, even though the contents were left untouched. I am in an unsettled period in my life.

JOSEPH, SYDNEY, AUSTRALIA

A: Walls represent exclusiveness and a desire to protect one's treasured possessions. It seems that your possessions inside the house are always unharmed, which suggests that possessions are a priority to you instead of how you face up to your family and friends. Ask yourself some strong questions about why you don't get the respect you deserve. Do you take and not give? When we see the outside of a house in a rundown state, this represents our persona – and that it is in need of some attention.

Q: I am 18 years old and I have this wonderful dream of a house that changes from dream to dream. I stand with the owner of the house on the ground floor and we know that on the top floor there is a beautiful hidden room that no one else knows about. We make our way up many staircases to get to the room. I feel so happy when I reach the secret room. In each dream, I seem to go different ways to get to this room.

AMANDA, IRELAND

A: Your dream is showing you the beauty within. Your knowledge of the whereabouts of the secret room indicates this clearly. Dream houses often consist of different levels – all performing different functions – connected to each other by stairs, doors and so on. Stairs often represent your sexual activities or desires. As you were taking different directions to reach your secret room, this shows how much you are changing and discovering yourself. Take stock of your ambitions and aspirations.

DIANA'S PREMONITION?

Understandably, the process of divorce often makes us feel vulnerable and alone – and Diana was no different. At around the time that the divorce was attracting publicity, Diana rang me soon after a dream that had greatly disturbed her.

I was in Australia at the time and it was the middle of the night when the phone rang. It was Diana calling from London. She spoke very quickly and urgently. 'Joan, I must tell you about this surreal dream I had last night. I'm seriously worried about it. I'm about to go to lunch with some friends to Daphne's, but I can't imagine myself sitting there and swapping gossip because I'm so overwhelmed by the terrible images in my dream.'

'Fire away,' I said, reaching for the notebook and pen I kept beside my bed, 'but go slowly as I want to take it all in.'

Diana loved Paris, but, in the dream she related to me, the city that she loved became a grotesque, surreal place. Buildings, like Notre Dame, seemed to be melting and loomed over her threateningly.

Diana began, 'I was walking along and I was absolutely tiny. The Seine was flowing so strongly it looked as if it was building to a tidal wave and all the bridges had disappeared. I kept walking and saw the Eiffel Tower – but it looked like a monstrous metal tombstone. In the dream, I knew that there were many people buried beneath it.' Her voice was frank and full of fear.

I stopped her. 'Slow down,' I said. 'I think that being tiny in your dream relates to your childhood. Everything seems so much bigger and more threatening to children. What disturbs me is that the Paris you love, a place where you feel so relaxed and in harmony, appears in this dream with such a strong sense of threat.'

'Joan, don't interrupt. There's much more I need to tell you,' she said impatiently. 'Even though I was scared, I walked towards the tower and there was a type of crypt. I could see a body in a sitting-up position; it looked like a ritual burying place. I turned and ran away quickly, but because I was so tiny I felt as if I couldn't run fast enough.

'Then, I was in a train that was chugging out of the Gare du Nord. Someone – a man – was urging me to jump out. Even though I was frightened of jumping from a moving train, I felt like this man was my protector. But he was tiny like me, like a small version of a grown man. He wore a suit. The door on the train opened, wind rushed in and I jumped. The man jumped off with me. I landed in a field in the countryside, but right at the edge of a cliff that formed one side of a type of canyon – is that the right word, Joan?'

I encouraged her to keep talking, knowing that she remembered this dream so vividly because she was not long awake from it. Although it was the middle of my night, I had turned on the light and I was scribbling notes while she spoke. Ironically, the notebook at my bedside was my own dream diary, and here I was noting Diana's dream in it!

'Paris was in the distance, on the other side of the canyon, and, for some reason, I knew we had to make our way back on foot. But how could we cross the canyon? Then I saw a strange structure bridging the abyss. I said to the small man, "What's that thing?" He said, "It's a rope bridge." We got up close to it and could see the rope was frayed and the walkway was made of old, splintered wood.'

I asked her if the bridge seemed ready to

collapse. 'Yes,' she replied, 'I was so scared. But the man urged me to crawl across it on all fours. He said something like, "For heaven's sake, Diana, get up and move quickly, don't you want to get back to Paris?"'

'And you wanted to go back to Paris, even though it had seemed so dreadful?' I probed.

'Yes, definitely,' she replied. 'I didn't even consider I had a choice in the matter.'

'And how did the dream end?' I encouraged her to go on.

'Well, I looked up and saw a train on the other side of the canyon and I wished I was on it. But then I saw it explode with a sharp cracking noise and a shrill whistling sound. This was what woke me and I lay very, very still for almost ten minutes. It was all so graphic.'

I knew what she meant because I, too, felt overwhelmed at first by the magnitude of the descriptions and images in this dream. When I asked her what her primary emotion had been on waking, she reported, bluntly, 'Fear.'

I followed my intuition and asked her if there were some secrets that she held that were troubling her.

She replied, 'Of course. I know things that some people think that I shouldn't. Is this why my dream is so filled with threat?'

'Perhaps,' I said. 'But let's look at the images and their symbolism before we get carried away, don't you think?'

Diana agreed, adding, 'But these images were so vivid and frightening.'

I began my analysis: 'This small man is really your other self. He was there to help you get through – a small "hero" within who was with you on your journey to make sure you were rescued. Now, the Seine building to a tidal wave…'

'Yes, I know, Joan, my emotions,' she interrupted.

'… and the missing bridges could signify the loss of a link between you and the past,' I continued. 'Something about loss has the potential to be overwhelming, emotionally. This may have something to do with changes in your life at present.'

'Yes, that feels right,' she replied.

'The fragile rope bridge you were crawling across possibly refers to the obstacles that are ahead for you. I worry about it because it indicates that you may have difficulties coming to terms with some of the things in your future.'

Diana asked what I meant by that.

'I'm not sure yet,' I answered, 'there are other significant images, too. Jumping from a moving train suggests that you will survive if you are not forced into a journey. The image of the Eiffel Tower, the crypt and the body are quite ghoulish, and – I hesitate to say this – seem quite premonitory. In any event, they are reminders of death and the limited lifespan that we all have. Perhaps this also relates to your marriage, but it is a very strong image.'

'I knew I didn't want to hear what you had to say,' she said with grim humour. 'I felt such fear and helplessness last night – do you know what I mean?'

I tried to reassure her: 'Not everything in the dream was negative. In fact, there are some very positive aspects. You land on the edge of a cliff but you don't fall over it; the train that you are not on explodes. We don't know whether you manage to crawl across the bridge, but you made a good, if very nervous, start.'

'Yes,' she agreed, 'but I can't get over the feeling of death and destruction that filled the dream.'

Privately, I was disturbed by this dream. While I regretted blurting out the possibility of premonitions to Diana over the phone, I felt that the dream definitely had premonitory overtones. But I reasoned it away. I decided that it depicted a combination of a difficult time in her life, her graphic imagination and the strength of her repressed rage at Charles.

CHAPTER 7

DI'S GUYS

'The ruling Passion be it what it will/
The ruling Passion conquers Reason still.'
ALEXANDER POPE

PRINCE Charles was alternately said to be 'concerned' and 'happy' about his ex-wife's new romances. 'If she is happy, then I am happy,' he is supposed to have said of her relationship with Dodi Fayed. Diana's taste in men was sometimes questionable but we always forgave her indiscretions. After all, there was something touching yet painful about her search for love with cads and bounders. As with her shyness and lack of academic qualifications, what at first appeared to be a defect – her inability to pick a good man – was by some mysterious alchemy transformed into a virtue.

DALLIANCES

Diana told me a dream about a yoga teacher that she'd had while she was still married to Charles. It was at a time when Charles and Diana were more or less leading separate lives. He had Camilla and Diana was, as she put it, being 'quite naughty', trying to find someone of her own to love. Although there were tales of gentlemen friends arriving at the palace undercover, Diana was well aware how closely she was watched by the media. She was always careful to shield her dalliances from the public's gaze – at least until she was formally divorced.

'I have had this fantasy-type dream about a guy with whom I have been doing yoga. He is a very, very close friend of mine,' she told me. As she said it, she rolled her eyes and had a huge smile on her face. 'I have made love with him, but not at the time when I had this dream. In fact, at that time I had to put him off. He'd become very horny during one of our yoga sessions; I told him I felt sexy, too, but I thought – being practical – that we should finish our yoga! Why am I always so practical?

'Anyway, in my dream, I am looking at him

during our yoga class and I don't feel anything for him at all. I can't tell him this because he expects me to be warm and sexy. He turns to me and says, "A real woman wants sex all the time and if she doesn't she must be frigid." I thought, "Wow, what's all this about?" Then the image changed and I was in a classroom ready to begin an exam. It was a foreign-language exam and the teacher is standing in front of the class speaking in French and Italian alternately. Then she left the room and I got my books out and I cheated by looking up the answers. I didn't finish the paper, as the teacher came back into the room, but she didn't see that I had cheated.

'Then the dream showed my yoga friend again. He was furious with me and I realised that I had been "cheating" him by pretending to be sexually attracted to him. I ask myself, "Why do I have to act like this? What is going on?"'

'You've answered the question for yourself,' I said. 'You're right on track with this dream analysis. But it also indicates where you are now, within yourself. You are on the cover of magazines all over the world, and almost every one of them portrays you as a young, sexy woman – that's what they want you to be and want all women to aspire to. But all women know that we can't be "sexy" all the time. It's a myth we cannot live up to – and shouldn't have to! I think your dream is telling you to look for more romance rather than sex.'

The 'dalliance' dream

It is essential to bear in mind that dreams, with their symbolic connotations, may use sex as a means of conveying a broader message. Many of my readers write to me with dreams in which sex is explicitly depicted. These dreams make interesting reading! Many of them feature people who are not partners in real life. Often these dreams are pleasurable, but sometimes they are disconcerting. If you dream of someone for whom you harbour a strong sexual desire, then the dream is enacting a fairly straightforward fantasy. Whether or not it is appropriate for you to imagine sex with this person is another issue. If you are in a monogamous relationship and your dreams are merely mirroring a conscious attraction, then you may need to have a long hard look at your primary relationship. Does the dream lover represent something that you are not receiving or giving? Is it time to re-evaluate? Often, dreamers in a perfectly harmonious relationship will enjoy erotic dreams featuring someone they know, but to whom they are not consciously attracted. In this case, it may be a simple acknowledgement of the fact that the dream partner may turn the dreamer on, in some subliminal way, or that the dream partner has a special quality that may be appealing.

Q: Recently, I have been having vivid dreams of watching my boyfriend make love to a woman I know. The dream started with both of us running our hands over his naked body. She then proceeded to make love to him. I can only describe the feeling as unbearable; it was like having someone die who was very close. The scary part was that I felt as if I deserved it. Afterwards, I took the woman home and was very nice to her, but, on returning to my boyfriend, I informed him I would not sleep with him for three months until he had an AIDS test. What could this mean? He is a wonderful man who would never cheat on me. We are both firm believers in our relationship. I have also been having dreams about being married to a horrible man, but at the same time having an affair with my current boyfriend. I love him very much, and to have such vivid dreams really scares me. I cannot look the woman from the first dream in the eye any more. Please help!

MEREDITH, SYDNEY, AUSTRALIA

A: In real life, it sounds as if your relationship is 'perfect', yet in your dreams you act out an opposite role. Your boyfriend was almost like a plaything for you and your female friend. Perhaps she has shown him attention or affection in real life. This sort of dream image often coincides with a real-life situation. In both of your dreams, you appear to be the instigator of the problem, and he becomes the vulnerable and unwitting partner. I wonder if you indulge in self-punishment fantasies. There is a sense of victimisation hanging over these dreams, so you should watch out for this in waking life.

SEX OBJECT

Diana had the following dream when she was visiting Pakistan. It is interesting to note that Diana's mother told her friends that she didn't approve of the Muslim men that Diana had been friendly with. Diana naturally was very angry when her mother voiced these opinions. Later, she even refused to accept her mother's apologies.

Diana told me, 'I have a dream about being chased by a group of men with swords and I find myself in a large room. I don't recognise anyone but one man has huge, big brown sad eyes, and I am reminded of a distant lover who seems to be further than ever away from me in his own beloved country which he will never leave, even though I live in hope that he will. I turn around to face the men and they plunge their swords into me, even the one who reminds me of my lover, whose sword then turns into a surgical instrument. I accept my death.

'Then the scene changes and I find myself alone in Highgrove. I hear crying and to my horror I think I have left a child locked in a garden shed and I must run and let her out. I am in a frenzy. I find the shed and unlock it. A beautiful little blonde girl of about ten rushes out, crying, and hugs me. I ask her if she's angry with me, but she tells me that she "is a big girl now", over and over again.

'I take her to a party and she is immediately the centre of attention. Everyone loves her as she tells them all tales of her adventures. I think how attractive and happy she seems, even after her ordeal, and I tell myself I am lucky to have found someone so lovely.'

I tell her, 'Your dream's message is very clear. The knives symbolise sexuality and show that you are fearless when you have chosen a partner. You accepted your "death" in your dream because the next image was your resurrection (the little girl was you). She was locked away because you had been locking away an important part of yourself – your vulnerable, spontaneous self. You do this, I suppose, when you are looking for love. A lot of us do. Let's face it, most women are brought up to consider themselves as sex objects. I think your dream ended really well. The little girl showed you who you really are and what you really want.'

Pursuit dreams

Being chased in a dream is usually associated with fear. Ask yourself what or who is pursuing you. What pressure do you need to alleviate? Dreams of being chased are common in childhood, and often the pursuer is a monster or scary animal. In adult dreams, these motifs may continue, or the pursuer may be a person, even the Shadow figure (see Chapter 2). The message is a strong one, and it is important to 'turn around' and face the fear. Dreamers who can do this report that they are able to confront and vanquish the pursuer once they examine the fear or pressure that it really represents.

Q: I have this dream where I am being chased by two men, each holding a knife. I am running very fast, holding a child in my arms. I have no idea who the child is and why I am running.

BELLA, WALES

A: Sometimes an out-of-control environment in your everyday life can lead to dreams where we are being pursued. What was happening in your life at the time of this dream? Running from something or someone is destructive to our sense of security. Perhaps you are failing to face something that is troubling you deeply. If this dream is recurring, make a mental note to try to 'face up' to your pursuers. I have found that if you are able to do this the dream will often fade, as it indicates that you have taken control.

DODI FAYED

Much has been said about whether Diana really loved Dodi Fayed. When she first began seeing him, she definitely told me, 'I've met someone.'

I spoke to Diana about Dodi's culture and the Arab approach to dreams.

I told Diana that Arab civilisation had produced dream dictionaries and lots of material devoted to dream interpretations. It is well known that the Koran reports that Muhammad rose from obscurity to found Islam after a divinely inspired dream.

Diana mentioned a time when she was on board the Fayeds' yacht, *Jonikal*, just off Portofino in Italy. She was very happy because she had the boys with her and they all had a marvellous time together. There was a contented family air among them. She told me, 'I did enjoy my sleep and my dreams then. It must be because I'm always so relaxed near the sea. And the people I was with made it easy as well. There was no pressure.'

She told me one of her dreams had been about Dodi. After having the dream, she teased him about it, as he was so thrilled and wanted to know what it had been about. 'I told him that in my dream he was dressed like Lawrence of Arabia and was riding a big black horse with

a pack of riders behind him. The strange thing
was that they weren't in the desert – they were
riding through somewhere like Times Square in
New York. I didn't recognise him at first in the
dream, but as the group came closer I realised it
was my Dodi. I was sitting in an oasis,
surrounded by high palm trees, and it was very
hot. Then the scene changed and I saw William,
my son, racing past me on a spaceship. He was
laughing and pointing at a line of men wearing
dark suits.

'I wanted to talk to William but he sped away
and disappeared. Then my dream turned back
to Dodi, who was coming towards me, laden
with fruits and golden boxes of jewels. All the
riders had presents for me, such as coconuts and
bananas. I was embarrassed and I didn't feel
comfortable because I wasn't prepared for such
a spectacle.'

'How did you feel when you woke up?'
I asked.

'Bewildered yet flattered; and liked and
loved, I suppose. I know I was embarrassed in
my dream but I wasn't when I woke up.'

I replied, 'Dodi and his father were no doubt

showering you and your children with attention and gifts at the time. William appeared, happy and racing around in his spaceship, which mirrored his happy demeanour during your holiday. All of this simple happiness and generosity would have pleased you; yet hovering over this happiness was your worry of always being watched by the "men in line".'

'Yes,' she replied. 'And when I told Dodi of this dream he said how much he loved giving me presents, but hadn't thought of giving me grapes and delicious fruits. He said he wanted to give me the world! The Fayed family had lots of toys and things for the boys to enjoy, too. That's probably why I saw William on the spaceship – I recall seeing him whizzing around on a sea scooter thing and having tremendous fun with it, even buzzing me in the water when I was swimming.' She then asked me, 'But what did it mean in my dream when I saw Dodi dressed like Lawrence of Arabia?'

'It means,' I answered, 'that his present giving and the way you were enjoying your holiday with his family felt "foreign" to you. It was something you weren't used to.'

Diana brightened. 'We do have so much in common and I love the fact that he spends all his time thinking about me and what we will do together. All the other men in my life have always done their own thing; I have never been the sole attraction in their lives. I know that I am with Dodi. I also feel protected and safe and I do enjoy the affection he shows me – I really love it because there's no secrecy about it. Until now, I'd always felt safer on my own instead of sharing my life, because of all the baggage that goes with being someone's partner.'

I told her it had probably been a long time since she had felt so happy being herself.

'Yes, it certainly has,' she replied.

When Diana returned from this holiday, she learned that Charles had appeared on a Channel 5 documentary, in which he claimed that he had 'never loved' his wife. This upset Diana. She knew he had loved her when they married. She was angry, too. It was something she didn't want her boys to hear their father say – especially on national television.

Gift dreams

Gifts are largely positive symbols in dreams. But if the dreamer is being given gifts and they are embarrassed by the largesse of the giver it can mean that the dreamer does not want someone's attention. If the gift is opened to reveal something disappointing, disgusting or trivial, then this would point to disappointment in a relationship that the dreamer holds dear. Giving gifts in dreams indicates our desire to be in a relationship with the receiver; it can also mean a deep yearning to feel liked or accepted by others. Jewels as gifts indicate that something in the relationship between giver and receiver is transformative in a positive sense.

Q: In my dream, I am in my office and sitting at my desk. A courier arrives with a package for me and I sign for it. It's a big parcel and I begin to open it slowly. I can distinctly hear the paper tearing as I unwrap it. But each time I take a layer of paper off there seems to be another one underneath. I can never see what is in the parcel. In the meantime, my colleagues come along and interrupt me, asking me questions about this and that. I carry on unwrapping, without getting anywhere. I wake up still not knowing what was in the parcel for me. What was in it? What does it mean?

KARL, CORNWALL

A: You are trying to unravel some hidden secrets or mysteries, probably in your workplace. It absorbs you to the extent that you cannot perform your mundane work activities. Your subconscious is telling you that unwrapping these secrets or mysteries may require a lot of perseverance.

CHAPTER 8

A FRAGMENTED FAMILY

'Consciousness reigns but does not govern.'
PAUL VALERY

DIANA'S childhood was described by her mother as one of happiness, where she had the opportunity to enjoy *two* loving homes with her pets and her sisters and brother. Two homes, because her mother divorced her father and they both remarried. Despite her mother's claims of a happy childhood, it is fair to say that Diana had problems with both of her parents, especially her mother. She also had a long-standing issue with her brother Charles. He had been brought up as the son and heir of an aristocratic family. By rights, he should have been the family 'star'. But Diana's fame easily eclipsed that of her brother, causing some tension between them.

DIANA'S FATHER

Diana dreamt about her loving father quite often and she always enjoyed her dreams of him. She said they reminded her of the special times they'd had together. Her dreams of him were rather strange yet quite typical of the kind of dreams we have about someone we love who has passed on (her father died in 1992).

One dream she often had was where she and her father were walking arm-in-arm through the grounds of their family home, Althorp. I told her these were called visitation dreams and were very common for people who had loved ones that had died.

She told me, 'He seemed so real in the dream. It sounds incredible, but I could even smell him. We laugh together and talk about everything, especially my boys. He asks how they are, how much they have grown – questions that any grandparent would ask.'

One of these dreams worried her. In it, all the trees around the garden had fallen over or been chopped down. 'In the dream,' she said, 'I told my father that I didn't approve that all our lovely, big shady trees had gone. Father just smiled at me and nodded. In that moment, I felt really happy just to have him to myself. After he married Raine, I never really felt the same when we were together.'

I told her what I thought of this dream: 'Trees always depict the father figure in dreams. The fact that they were cut down – and so unable to grow back again – symbolised your father's death. The severing of the trees perhaps also indicates that you felt severed from your spiritual roots, your family. When you dream of your father, remember that he is there to share and talk with you, and to heal, too.'

She told me that in her dreams her father told her that he didn't think that she was the shy, demure girl the press made her out to be. He told her that she was made of steel underneath it all – and thank goodness for that, because she was going to need to be strong. He also told Diana how much he admired her.

'I mostly dream of him each year around my birthday,' she told me.

I said this was interesting, as we all have a yearly moon that arrives to each of us around our birthday, and that this moon influences dreaming.

Another visitation dream Diana had came when she heard about the death of Princess Grace of Monaco in a car accident. Diana admired Princess Grace. When they first met, they found they had a lot in common and a connection formed between them. Diana even had a gown that she loved that she called her Grace Kelly dress. Diana even went to Princess Grace's funeral alone. The rest of the royal family was holidaying at Balmoral.

As for the dream, she told me that it was both funny and sad at the same time. 'Princess Grace and I were in a lovely minimalist kitchen. Neither of us spoke. Princess Grace had her hair pulled back in a ponytail and was wearing gym clothes. She looked fit and terrific. I sat on a high stool as I watched Princess Grace busy herself. Without looking at me, she held out a jug of carrot juice. I couldn't believe it, as I love that drink so much. I took the jug and placed it in front of me on the work surface. I don't know why, but it seemed really important to me that we were in that shiny, spare kitchen.

'The weird thing was that Princess Grace seemed to keep fading in and out, like a ghost – or maybe it was just the spirit of her that was there. It wasn't a particularly disturbing or affecting dream, but I thought I would mention it because dreaming of her after she died was like my dreaming of my father after his death. I didn't remember this dream until someone offered me some carrot juice at breakfast the next day. I was gobsmacked. I said to myself, "That was Princess Grace in my dream. What was she doing there?"'

I told her, 'We often see people that have passed on in our dreams. They pop up sometimes because we are still grieving for them, or because we see a picture of them or someone reminds us of them. As the dream was set in a kitchen, its message may have been for you to "nourish" yourself – especially as she offered you your favourite drink. She may also have been spoiling you a little. It could have been her way of thanking you for coming to her funeral.'

Visitation dreams

Visitation dreams are usually connected to a strong emotional bond between the dreamer and the person they dream of. Often these dreams have an element of telepathy. Twins, for example, often report dreaming accurately of events happening to each other, even if they are not in contact at the time. Close relatives or family members may dream of each other, particularly if a warning of some sort, or a cry for help, is implied in the dream. Dreams of people who are dead may be equally distressing. To a large extent, they form part of the grieving process, allowing the dreamer to come to terms with loss. There may be a feeling of guilt involved: perhaps the dreamer did not have time to say 'goodbye' to the dead loved one, or held repressed resentment which was never aired. In these cases, and if the dream is persistent and troubling, I suggest the dreamer confronts the problem and lets out the guilt – for example, by writing a letter to the person in the dream, or visiting the grave site. In any case, it is most important to address the uncomfortable emotions that are dredged up.

Q: I often dream of my brother, who died in an accident in 1991. I dream of seeing him fit and healthy and he is smiling at me and is very calm. I try to run to him but find I cannot move. I often wake up crying after these dreams.

BROOKE, EDINBURGH

A: Recurring dreams that depict a visitation from a deceased loved one are dreams of reassurance. They can also relate to the period of grieving after death. The image of you being unable to reach him relates to part of your own grieving process; when you understand this, the dream will not be so upsetting. Maybe you did not see him prior to the accident. This adds more weight to the visit in your dream. Try to accept these dreams as happy and positive – your brother is smiling, after all. These dreams are messages from your subconscious telling you that your brother is still there to share your feelings with – if not in body, then definitely in spirit.

Q: I was fortunate to have 14 years of wonderful companionship with my dear wife, Nan. She died 12 months ago, after I had nursed her through illness for three years. On the anniversary of her death, I had a dream in which she came into my room. It was so real. She told me she was all right. I asked her, twice, what it was like on the other side but she didn't reply. I felt wonderful after the dream.

TED, STRATFORD

A: We don't usually keep dream diaries in the same way that we keep daily diaries, but visitation-type dreams do often follow anniversary patterns. They tend to occur either on the anniversary of a loved one's death or on a date commemorating valued or special time between the dreamer and the deceased.

DIANA'S BROTHER

One day, I was explaining to Diana how the language a person uses can influence the images in their dreams. 'If you regularly call someone or something "really hot", or "hot stuff",' I said, 'it can lead you to have a "hot" dream.' I asked her if she had experienced any 'hot' dreams, as they could be connected to her love life.

She told me she hadn't had any recently: 'Charles is the love of my life. No matter what happens, he is the only man I've ever wanted to be with forever, and that's not going to happen now.'

Then she did recall one heat-related dream: 'I was looking at a huge country mansion. It was covered in mist and cloud – and when the cloud lifted I realised that it was my home, Althorp. People were running everywhere and it seemed as if a show was going on. Then I saw these giant rings of fire surrounding the property. I wasn't worried about the fire; I just wondered why I hadn't been invited to join in. At that moment, I noticed who was leading the crowds of people: it was my brother, Charles.' She told me that she hadn't wanted to bring up this dream, as she and her brother were not getting on at that point.

'Anyway, there he was. He was dictating to everyone around him what they had to do. It was like a circus, somehow, and he seemed to be a circus ringleader.

'It was quite comical. My brother had hardly any clothes on and he was built like a body-builder, with rippling muscles and strong thighs. As I watched, like a voyeur, he took out a can of drink and pulled open the ring, which he offered to me. I took the ring and put it on my finger and laughed. Then the dream changed and became dark and threatening. I woke up sweating. I glanced down at my hand and wondered where the ring had gone. It had been a very real dream.'

'The images in your dream are quite remarkable,' I said. 'While fire in dreams is often indicative of some kind of attraction, in this case I think it represented a more generic feeling of warmth and love, as well as anger, too. The fact that you received a pretend ring from him and that he looked extremely masculine may indicate a desire on your part to make up with the person who, following your father's death, had become the head of the family.

Fire in dreams

Fire is a powerful but ambivalent dream symbol. Fire destroys but, at the same time, it also cleanses and purifies. In dreams, it can signal a new beginning, or it can be associated with disruptive emotions – perhaps the flames of passion and envy or rage. Fire in dreams may suggest a need for a sacrifice, but at the same time promises to open up new opportunities. Fire is a masculine energy and it represents that which is overt, positive and conscious. Out of control, however, it suggests the need for the dreamer to take better charge of unbridled passion or ambition.

Q: In my dream, I look through a window into my back garden and see that the house next door is burning furiously. I gather my children around me and ask them to collect their belongings, including their pets. Suddenly, the fire jumps the fence and my garden is on fire, with small explosions all over the place, like fire crackers. I search for a hose and then firemen arrive. I try to help but the fire gets out of control. My house catches fire and collapses. I cry tears of anger and frustration as I watch everything I own being destroyed. I awake feeling really angry.

BRONWYN, BATH

A: The fire in your building is a metaphor for the anger you are harbouring in your body. The fire that consumes and destroys all your belongings, but not you or your family, signifies that you are in need of a purification of sorts. Are you overly concerned with material possessions? Or, perhaps you have fallen on hard times and you are losing your possessions or need things that you cannot have. In any event, your family is protected and you must take comfort from that. Try to work through and eliminate this anger as the fire shows you how destructive it can be.

DIANA'S MOTHER

Throughout her life, Diana had many, many dreams about her mother.

Even though in dream symbolism the mother figure represents nurturing, fertility and loving care, as we grow up a darker side to this figure can appear – that of a possessive and overbearing female, such as we often read about in fairy stories: the wicked stepmother or the witch.

Diana told me about a strange dream she had of two telephones. There was a red telephone and a black telephone. They were in the kitchen of a large farmhouse, the red one on top of a stove and the black one balancing precariously on a windowsill. She told me, 'The red one rang and when I tried to answer it I couldn't reach it; when the black one rang I reached it, but it fell off the windowsill. I picked up the receiver but no one was there.'

In the dream, she checked the phone connections to make sure they were working. She felt menaced by the phones in some way. There was no one else in the kitchen, which she said was a bright, pleasant room with a nice atmosphere.

I reminded Diana that she told me she had been having some recent disagreements with her mother. She had been especially reluctant to return her mother's phone calls as they usually ended in an argument. 'Arguments aggravate me,' she said.

'Perhaps,' I told her, 'you feel guilty about not always being there for your mother when she calls. The dream is set in the warmth of a kitchen, which suggests your nourishing self in dream symbolism. Communicating with your mother may be difficult and you may often misunderstand each other. However, the message from your dream is to try to be patient and happy when you communicate with other members of your family.'

In another dream, Diana saw her mother in the corner of her bedroom looking at her. The figure was identifiably her mother, but when she spoke she had the fangs of a vampire. I must point out that this dream occurred when Diana was extremely vulnerable and trying desperately to set up a life for herself after her divorce.

These dreams are extremely distressing and they are related to the mother being bigger and stronger and very frightening at times during our childhood. As we become adults, the dreams related to our mother begin to change, yet she often remains a mystery. Diana's mother left the family home when Diana was six years old and, no doubt, Diana was carrying some guilt about this occurrence from her childhood.

In another dream, Diana felt very violent towards her mother. She said the dream was taking place in her home, but it was colourless and confused. She sensed that the figure towards whom she was feeling so much violence in the dream was her mother, even though it didn't look like her.

I asked her what she meant by 'being violent' and she said it was her mood in the dream. She said she was in a really bad mood and she felt violent towards herself. I asked Diana if she did anything violent in the dream, such as push or punch or kick.

'No,' she replied, 'it was just a feeling of violence.'

Diana said that when she woke up she felt she had been fighting or destroying something or someone. Her mother was the first person she thought of after waking.

'If Freud were here,' I said, 'he would no

doubt say that you were feeling guilty about something to do with your mother at the time of the dream. He would probably also comment on the fact that you never easily accepted the authority of your parents.'

Diana replied, 'But why did I have this sort of dream?'

I asked her to think about the day of the dream and whether she'd had a discussion with her mother or anyone else in her family.

She said she'd had a conversation with her mother the day before the dream. She told me, 'It's often difficult having conversations with my mother.'

Violence in dreams

Violence in a dream often appears at a distance, especially if the dreamer is committing the act of violence. The emotional ambience may remain neutral and detached. This seems to imply that the dream's messages relate to conflict of another kind, such as differences in opinion in the dreamer's mind, or some unresolved anger. When the dreamer is the victim of violence, then life conflicts are signalled. Do you have escalating debts? Is your health good? Are you in a threatening situation in any way at work or emotionally? Finding yourself in a war zone in your dreams depicts a need for reconciliation rather than victory over what you perceive to be the 'enemy' in the dream. When the dream represents self-violation, then this can signal guilt or a desire for self-punishment.

Q: There were many children in my dream, enjoying themselves in a playground. I went into the playground and began to push the children off the swings. Then, I kept pushing the swings too high for the children to climb back on to them. There was a roundabout, too, and I would not let the children play on that either. I felt so upset when I woke up. I love my children; I love all children. I'm not like that at all in real life. Please help.

SOL, TASMANIA, AUSTRALIA

A: This dream represents your inability to face and accept your own 'child' within.

You may be experiencing a time of readjustment of identity. Have your circumstances changed recently? You could be finding differences of opinion or resentments difficult to accept. Dreaming of violence towards children gives you a strong message to sort out any conflicts that may seem 'childish' to you.

CHAPTER 9

RULING IN HER OWN RIGHT

'All dreams of the soul/End in a beautiful man's or woman's body.'

W B YEATS

WHEN Diana's 'Her Royal Highness' title was withdrawn after her divorce, her son William said to her, 'Don't worry, Mummy, I will give it back to you when I am king.' Her thoughts for herself and her boys were always paramount. She was always planning and looking to their future. She wanted William to be made of the 'right stuff' to be able to cope with the rigours of palace officialdom. She was ambitious for them and always wanted her boys to be able to reach out to their father and to the monarchy. She had a lot in common with Dodi and she delighted in his company and regarded meeting him as a new adventure for both her and her boys.

THE QUEEN OF HEARTS

I was with Diana at Kensington Palace one day, just before she was due to visit her friends Imran and Jemima Khan in Pakistan. She was excited about the trip and we spent a lot of time discussing what she would wear. She told me that she loved to wear the *Shalwar Kameez*, Pakistan's national dress.

There was a wonderful itinerary booked for her and she had a lot on her mind – as usual!

She told me, 'Joan, there is this amazing dream that has been following me around now for a while.' In the dream, she was standing in a shallow lake and at one end of it was a huge statue of the Ancient Egyptian queen Nefertiti (she knew it was Nefertiti, as she had seen her image in the British Museum). On either side of the statue were two enormous sphinxes. She seemed to glide straight past them and then, suddenly, she was up close to them.

Diana described how Nefertiti was dressed.

She laughed as she told me, 'She looked like a pop star. She was wearing a full wig, which was green, and had a jewelled scarf around her head. It looked like an ornamental headdress in the form of vulture wings. She also had on a long white dress with an Egyptian frilled collar and matching armbands, and in one hand she carried what seemed to be a stick of some sort.

'But the amazing thing was that she had black skin. I was shocked by this because I always imagined the Egyptians to have white or fairer skin.

'I gazed at these three monuments beside the lake and felt an amazing sense of calm and peace. Then the dream changed to me sinking slowly under the lake and when I came up the monuments were gone. I know I am off to Pakistan soon and I wondered if the foreignness of my trip influenced this dream. The images were divine, but I'm not going to Egypt. So why the sphinxes?'

I replied, 'It seems to me that you had a sort of baptism in your dream. You were at the altar of the Egyptian gods and in the lake the water was peaceful and shallow. You had no fear when you were immersed in the water, which to me sounds like a ritual. All I can say is that this dream definitely has a message for you and it is related to a re-birth or a transformation of how you feel spiritually. Was Nefertiti's skin black in the painting you remember?'

'Yes,' she replied, 'but in the dream it seemed even darker.'

I said, 'This suggests fertility and re-birth. Maybe it's because you are on your way to Pakistan, where religious belief is much more pronounced than here. It even influences what people wear. I know you are going to wear the *Shalwar Kameez* during your visit and this will be appreciated by your hosts. It shows consideration on your part, and a desire to make those around you feel comfortable.'

Diana accepted this. 'I do love people to feel themselves around me, and this trip has been quite controversial, to say the least. The powers-that-be don't want me to go, as Pakistan isn't seen as a politically correct place to visit. I've pointed out to them that this is a private visit. I organised the trip with Jemima to support the hospital that Imran is building for cancer victims. It is the only hospital of its kind in Pakistan. But dodging the hierarchy has become quite a habit of late. They don't want me to appear on television over there or make any public speeches. I won't, but by just being there it will generate a lot of worldwide interest in Imran and Jemima's hospital project. They are both so loved by the people of Pakistan. Did you know that, as I've been called the "Queen of Hearts" here, so Jemima is called the same thing in Pakistan. We're the two Queens of Hearts!'

She continued, 'I've really been thinking a lot recently about what makes me tick. I think this trip could make the Foreign Office notice me and that I could ultimately become some sort of ambassador for Great Britain. I really want this trip to be a triumph.'

I told her, 'Your dream shows maturity and spiritual strength. I sure that this dream heralds a growing sense of freedom and wisdom within you.'

When I think back about Diana's dream of

submerging herself in the lake, my thoughts take me to the little island that is the monument to Diana at her home in Althorp. It did occur to me that the original lake in Althorp had to be recontoured and lowered to allow for the construction of Diana's memorial.

'Big' dreams

These are so called because they signify a big change or shift in the psyche of the dreamer. They are also called archetypal dreams. These dreams are often recalled with great clarity. Another characteristic of these dreams is that the dreamer feels that they have received wisdom from a 'higher' source. The symbols in big dreams may not correspond with any waking-life people or emotions but they carry with them a sense of great significance. There is something about big dreams that inspire a sense of awe in the dreamer. Some sort of journey often figures in these dreams as well as a wise figure with either human or animal characteristics.

Q: In my dream, I am travelling across a wide, hot plain. In the distance is some sort of house, very large and sprawling. The area is barren, no trees or foliage as I walk towards this place, which I have a sense in the dream is where I must be, like my home. I finally get there and before I reach the door I have to wade through miles and miles of wheat – it's blowing in my face and the sun is shining in a bright-blue sky. The whole setting seemed to have completely changed. As I go inside the house, I look up and there is no roof, the sun shines down on me. The walls are lined with bookcases and at the very top of one – where the roof should be – is a large eagle's nest, with an eagle perched in it.

I go to step further into the house and see a huge dark-blue pond. Beside the pond is a dark but fascinating man – dressed in flowing robes – he has a fishing line and I say, 'There can't be fish in there,' but he just nods and throws in his line. He gets a bite and begins to reel in his line, but the fish seems too heavy and he drops the line and uses his hands. Suddenly, at my feet is an enormous golden fish. So golden!

The man has a big knife and he starts to cut it up, on the floor of this roofless house. It feels amazing. I turn around and there is a crowd of people and he gives pieces of the fish to everyone. The man seems to be hypnotised by the fish. This dream has stayed with me for a long time. When I woke up, I just lay there in my bed and stared in wonderment at my ceiling!

NATASHA, DUBLIN

A: Your dream has such beauty and spirituality. The symbols in your dream signify an excellent future for you. Walking across the plain into a field of wheat depicts abundance and plenty. The eagle is associated with power and height and the spirit. The books are indicators of learning and the deep blue waters of the pool show your deep emotions. The fish is the mystic ship of life and being golden it becomes the 'cosmic' fish connected to the universe. The man was your spiritual guide, endowed with the culture of his forebears. I think you will be able to travel to the ends of the earth and you will be able to surmount any of life's trials with strength and spirituality.

DIANA THE MOTHER

Because Diana and I loved to talk about our children, it was no surprise when she told me one night of a dream she'd had about William. It had been when William was a small boy, just after Harry's birth.

Diana said that her whole being revolved around her boys and that she loved to be with them more than with anyone. Her only concern was that she and Charles would now be separate parents and, of course, Diana had always wanted to have a perfect family. She had always envisaged herself growing up to become a mother. She had no idea that her life would take such an unexpected twist and that she would indeed become a mother after all – to the future King of England.

In these circumstances, it was quite understandable that Diana dreamt about her children. All mothers do. They come to identify with their children, their needs and wants, and loves and hates.

At the time of this particular dream, Diana's relationship with Charles was extremely strained. She knew by this time that their marriage was over.

In Diana's dream, she saw William crossing a very large bridge with water surging by on both sides. He crossed the bridge easily and then jumped into a chariot that was waiting nearby. The horses pulling the chariot started slowly but then began to race. The chariot looked as if it was about to turn over. Then, a tiger bounded into view, running beside the chariot, which began to slow down. 'William wasn't afraid,' she told me. 'He was relaxed and enjoying the energy of the horses and the tiger. The tiger jumped up on to the seat beside him and put his large paw on Wills's shoulder.'

'How did you feel after this dream?' I asked.

Diana took a breath and said, 'Well, I wasn't

frightened for him, strangely enough. The tiger was very beautiful and was more like a big dog than a frightening animal.' She asked me what the dream meant.

'Your son was in control,' I told her. 'No doubt he will be a strong leader of his country one day. You dreamt this dream at a time when you were moving away from his father, and this is your subconscious's way of showing you that you believe in your son and his future. Your dream showed him in charge and in control, and raised up in a prestigious position. He crossed the river easily and was befriended by a fierce tiger, which represents strength and valour in the service of righteousness. The tiger can be both the wild beast and the tamed animal – a gorgeous creature to have in one's dream.'

Tiger dreams
Like the lion, the tiger represents animal passions that can either devour or create natural order. The tiger is also the ruler of his domain, the jungle. He is regal and courageous, and stands for mastery, the sun

and masculinity. In Chinese mythology, the tiger represents both cruelty and darkness, as well as valour and protection. The dreamer needs to look to his or her passions and maybe to tame the tiger within.

Q: In my dream, I was walking from my house to the pub with an ex-girlfriend. We passed a bungalow and through the window we saw a tiger walking around the living room. Neither of us made any comment. We had a drink at the pub and then walked back home. At the bungalow I stopped and looked at the tiger, which looked back at me. My ex said, 'Ignore it.' The next day, I went to see the tiger and told my friends, 'If you believe it won't hurt you then it won't hurt you!' My ex said, 'It'll kill you.' I walked over to the open window and the tiger put his front paws on the sill and his huge head in front of me. His amber eyes were full of love and he raised a giant paw and put it on my head – I felt so safe. He jumped through the window and I played with him like a little boy with his pet dog.

JULIAN, ESSEX

A: What a lovely dream! Your ex has been trying to suppress the tiger within you – so it's a good thing that you are no longer with this person. The tiger is an animal that is handsome, but can be fierce and terrifying. It often represents the male principle. Your tiger was loving and playful, and also protective. You mentioned elsewhere in your letter that you have responsibility for your teenage daughters, who live with you and not their mother. Is their mother the ex of your dream? If so, this dream shows that you can be the 'tiger' of your family, despite the misgivings of your former partner. You tamed the fierce tiger just as you will harness the power of your masculinity to love and protect your girls. The dream also suggests that you must encourage the playful side of yourself. Certainly, you will be able to survive anything if you keep your tiger dream close.

HER HERO

Diana described a beautiful young man from one of her dreams. She had this dream on a couple of occasions. I called him her Hero. Many women's dreams feature their 'dream' man. He is kind, thoughtful and loving and it seems in the dream that he will be with the dreamer forever. The dreamer reports a feeling of ecstasy in his presence. Diana had these feelings, too, when she dreamt of her Hero. When she saw his eyes in her dream she felt a sense of ecstasy more powerful than any she had ever known. She told me that when she awoke and realised it was all a dream her disappointment was almost unbearable.

I told her that this type of dream is very common. Although it seemed upsetting, it really symbolises that falling in love is something that is built into all of our lives. It is a hopeful and positive dream: it is showing you that you can love, even if you don't have anyone to love right now.

In Diana's Hero dream, she and her lover were flying. 'Just soaring with arms out-stretched,' she told me, 'it felt so delicious.'

Flying dreams

Flying symbolises ambition, achievement and freedom and is often associated with sexual joy. Peak sexual experiences may induce, or be induced by, flying dreams. These dreams are often experienced by people in the public eye or prominent business positions, as these sorts of people have a subliminal need to 'stay on top'. It is also reportedly a common dream for disabled people. In this case, flying offers them the freedom they do not have during waking hours.

Q: In my dream, I start off by taking two or three strides then launch myself into the air. I then glide slowly above the ground at a level of about 50 feet, with my arms usually in the crucifix position. Hand movements control flight direction and altitude. The location of these flights varies but it is always to a place I have

191

been before, sometimes many years ago. The people in the dream are not in any way familiar. And they seem to regard my floating as nothing unusual, sometimes smiling and waving. I then leave the area but I am now flying at great speed. I always head towards a mountain (shrouded in very dark clouds). The mountain is shaped like Japan's Mount Fuji. Just after I enter the clouds, I feel intensely cold. I then wake up shivering.

ROBERT, LINCOLNSHIRE

A: Your experience in this dream is related to your sexuality and the fact that you cannot bear the thought of losing control. Flying signifies ambition and sexual process as well as a sense of freedom. The feeling of great speed and flying towards a mountain is a description of you reaching your peak. The cold and shivering you felt is associated with your inability to reach the peak of the mountain and the solitude of your dream experience.

Q: I had a dream that my husband and I were at a motel with two of our married friends. There was a swimming pool at the motel and my friend's husband was lying down on a sun bed at the far end of the pool. I dived into the pool and swam to the end and then got out and sat next to him. We were talking and then all of a sudden we started kissing passionately. It was such a beautiful feeling. We were just about to sneak to a room when I woke up. I can't stop thinking of this dream but I don't understand it, as I love my husband very much.

JULIE, SYDNEY, AUSTRALIA

A: The location of your dream is suggestive and the fact that you dived into the water to reach your friend's husband shows your ability to plumb the depths of your emotions. Perhaps you find your friend's husband attractive, although dreams are not usually that literal. It might just be that you have noticed your friends have an intimacy that you feel you lack.

Perhaps you need reassurance from your husband. Maybe you need to show him more affection. Put TLC on the shopping list for both of you.

ACCEPTING HER NATURAL SELF

Diana was in a light-hearted mood when she told me about her dream of standing naked before a window that was veiled by a sheer curtain with butterflies stitched on it. As she looked down at herself, she saw that the pattern of the butterflies had fallen across her body. 'It was truly very beautiful,' she said. 'My body looked like a painting.'

I told her that Freud's favourite dream was one where he saw himself standing naked at a bus stop amid a queue of people who didn't even notice him. 'To dream of being naked,' I said, 'is to see oneself totally exposed. I think that your dream has connected you to your true spirituality and your natural self.'

Diana went on to say that in the dream she had felt warm, despite being naked.

I explained: 'That represents your purity. The window perhaps symbolises both your knowledge of the outside world and your need for self-examination. Also, the window in dreams is often associated with feminine sexuality. And I feel that the warmth on your body was a form of divine energy. How do you feel about that?'

Diana was delighted. 'I love it,' she said. 'I loved that dream.'

Naked dreams

Dreaming of being naked when others are fully dressed has nothing to do with sex. It is associated more with a feeling of exposure. When people act normally to the naked dreamer, this adds a sense of confusion to the feelings of the dream.

Q: Over the past ten years, I have had this recurring dream that starts with me getting ready for work. My make-up, my hair, everything done, I get to work and I don't have anything on from the waist up and I'm wearing jeans. People speak to me normally and nobody tells me that I am topless. I don't try to cover myself up.

BETH, LANCASHIRE

A: Are you in danger of being exposed as a fraud at work? Perhaps you are overly conscientious, and this is an irrational fear. Are you very prim and proper and need to loosen up? Or are you quite provocative in your everyday life? Whatever the reason, I'd say that you are very proud of your breasts!

Q: In my dream, I'm in a sort of building that looks like the school that my daughter goes to. I find two dead bodies and suddenly realise that I am totally naked. I try to hide as people are approaching but there's nowhere to go. Then I am in a grassy place, riding a horse. I try to make the horse go one way but he won't be directed by me. Two people I sort of recognise go past me but they don't seem to notice my nakedness.

ROSIE, SYDNEY, AUSTRALIA

A: The message from your dream is that you feel vulnerable, perhaps as vulnerable as you felt in childhood in front of

196

schoolyard bullies, and feel that taking control of your horse – and your life – is a bit more than you can handle. Assert yourself.

CHAPTER 10

DID DIANA DREAM HER OWN DEATH?

'And one day there will come a great awakening when we shall realise that life itself was a great dream.'

CHUANG-TZU

DIANA was a highly intuitive woman who I believe may have dreamt about her own death, which took place following a car crash in Paris in August 1997. In the days following Diana's death, there was an extraordinary worldwide outpouring of grief. We had lost a true fairy-tale princess. It was an event that has continued to haunt the collective unconscious of our times.

THE COFFIN
Diana had a dream in which there was a prominent image of a cemetery ready to receive a coffin. She said that the grave was surrounded

199

by vine leaves and as she looked down into it she saw a figure with the face of a very close friend and confidante. At the time of the dream, Diana's relationship had cooled towards this particular friend. Nevertheless, she was very worried about the dream.

I said to Diana that this dream image symbolised neglect. 'Quite a few of my dreamers have had this dream,' I said, 'and they are often terrified when they see the image of someone they love laid out in a grave.'

I told her that neglect of our loved ones can trigger this dream – the subconscious tends to overdramatise, but the message is clear: stay in touch!

As we talked at length about the friend in Diana's dream, I realised what opposites they were. Diana, cool and charming, quiet and dignified, warm to those that she trusted and to strangers in need, but mostly alone in the palace; her friend, bold and competitive with Diana and well liked by the royal family.

By the time we ended this conversation, Diana was feeling much more confident. She felt less threatened by her friend's strong position and confident demeanour and was ready to call her and resume their friendship once more.

Death or coffin dreams

Dreams of death are not literal. They may refer instead to neglect or to the 'dying off' of a part of oneself or relationships. Death often points to a sense of loss or abandonment. In almost all cases, death dreams prefigure change and transformation in the dreamer's life or relationships. Here is a 'death' dream that I myself had:

> I had just been diagnosed with breast cancer. The night before I was due to go into hospital for a mastectomy I dreamt – in perfect black and white – about an obituary column. I quickly looked it up and down for my name or any names of my family. None was there. Naturally, I received such confidence from that dream. My operation went on to be completely successful. That was nearly six years ago.

THE FUNERAL

On one of my visits to Kensington Palace, Diana told me about a dream she'd had a couple of times. She believed it to be a dream about the Queen Mother's funeral.

In the dream, Diana saw a huge contingent of royalty and VIPs from around the world converging on a church. She was amazed at the abundance of flowers stretching as far as the eye could see, fresh and beautiful flowers with little notes attached. She was surprised that Charles and her boys were not dressed as formally as everyone else. They were wearing lounge suits and she was puzzled because she knew how much preparation went into the planning and procedures of a royal funeral.

At the time of these dreams, Diana was only weeks away from her divorce. While I understood how Diana connected the dream to the death of the Queen Mother, I interpreted it as symbolising the death of Diana's marriage. I told her, 'Seeing a funeral symbolises the end of an era in our daily life.'

The flowers depicted her positive thoughts and wishes for her future. Charles and the boys in lounge suits possibly expressed her sense of them as a family – not a royal family, but her own family.

But in the light of her untimely death, I now believe that these were premonition dreams. Diana was seeing her own funeral.

About a year after Diana's death, I met with her close friend, confidant and butler, Paul Burrell. We spent a couple of hours together talking about Diana and how much we missed her. I told Paul about Diana's dream and he revealed to me that Diana had discussed it with him, too. Paul had never thought that the dream represented Diana's own funeral.

It was only after this meeting with Paul that I was really able to grieve for Diana. Until then, I'd found it extremely difficult to believe that she was dead.

Premonition dreams

There are two very special dreams that do come true: the premonition dream and the telepathic dream. The premonition dream is one in which the unexpected events dreamt actually occur at a later date. The telepathic dream depicts a person that the dreamer has no way of knowing anything about.

There is much historical evidence to suggest that premonitory and telepathic dreams happen regularly. Many ancient cultures revered the ability to dream in this way. However, to dream in this way is really very rare. Nowadays, we would treat most people who talk about 'seeing' events in their dreams with a large dose of scepticism. Nevertheless, these types of dreams do exist.

It has been argued that premonition and telepathic dreams are more commonly dreamt by women. Perhaps women are more open to unconscious messages than men. Accompanying symptoms, such as headaches, have been reported by many who dream of the future.

A record of the day's activities, prior to the prediction or telepathic dream, is most important, as it can offer the dreamer important clues. It may be that the premonition or telepathic message is really something connected with the day's activities or concerns, coupled with underlying concerns to which the dreamer is subject. So-called telepathic dreams are known to flourish if the dreamer is taking medication or drugs of any kind.

When two people have a similar dream they may share a sort of internal radar. Other predictions in dreams relate to luck – for example, winning the lottery. Dreams involving numbers are often experienced by those who encourage their highly intuitive powers.

Q: Nearly 12 years ago, I was feeling very depressed so I thought I would write out the invitations to our daughter's wedding to brighten myself up – which I did. That night, I dreamt that I had to cross my husband's name off the invitation list. Two weeks later, my husband suddenly died. I must admit that afterwards I was very scared to go to sleep in case I had more dreams like that.

KELLIE, SYDNEY, AUSTRALIA

A: Your premonitory dream occurred due to the emotional closeness that you enjoyed with your husband. Sceptics would say that it's hard to say whether the dream foresaw his death – although it certainly conveyed a very powerful image. You didn't mention whether your husband had been in perfectly good health or under stress that only he knew about. If he had been in a fit condition, then your dream was a premonition. If you had sensed a disorder in him of some kind, such as his colouring or changes in his appearance, then your dream was telepathic. You did mention that you were depressed when you went to write out the invitations and I wonder why. What is interesting is your ability to listen from within. You have an inner voice and your senses are tuned to be alert. But do try to listen for the good – as well as bad – messages and feelings. Unless you had shown a long predisposition to dreams of this nature, it would be unlikely that you would dream like this again.

Q: I would like to tell you about my dreams because a number of them have come true at a later date. Some events even happen the following day. The dreams are more like visions. I will describe one of them to you. It was approximately two years ago. At the time of the dream, I was married, but we were having problems. I had a dream of a man I had never met. I could see his clothes but his face was blacked out. My son was sitting between us and we were driving a truck. My son looked out of the window and said, 'There's my school.' I turned to the man and said, 'Remind me that I need to pay my horse-stabling fees.' I did not own a horse at the time. About eight months ago, my husband and I broke up and I started another relationship. My boyfriend, my son and I went for a drive one night. My son had started school just down the road from where I live, and I had bought a horse just before I broke up with my husband. On this particular night, we drove past the school and my son repeated what he said in the dream. I then turned to my boyfriend and asked him to remind me to pay my horse-stabling fees. At that moment, I remembered my dream. I turned to my boyfriend and said, 'Oh, it was you!' Of course, he had no idea what I was talking about. This sort of thing has happened to me many times. Often, I'm not even asleep when I experience these visions of the future.

GRETA, NEW SOUTH WALES, AUSTRALIA

A: Premonition dreams are quite common, even when the subject matter is relatively insignificant. Your brain has the ability to run ahead and give you a clear picture of an event in the future. This happens in a similar way to the phenomenon known as 'déjà vu' – which is when we experience something happening that we feel we have seen before, possibly in a dream. The difference is that one really is a dream and the other is a fleeting sense of memory.

EPILOGUE

TOWARDS the end of writing this book, I had a marvellous dream of a bee. This bee was buzzing and building a hive around a single light globe. It was building the hive in shining gold, in the shape of a crown. On waking, I was left with the image of myself, walking back and forth in the room, occasionally looking beneath the tiny globe to watch the bee at work. And I could still hear the faint sound of buzzing...

The dream's message was wonderful. It kept me going through the final, difficult stages of writing. The little bee was me, industrious and creative, building a shining monument as a beacon for the future. Just what I needed.

Diana also knew that her dreams were sending her important messages that could help on her life journey. She was a princess – but also a person who was trying to make sense of the world around her, just as we all are. Her dreams show that she was struggling with the same issues that you and I struggle with. I know that she would have wanted her legacy to be continued in this way – to help others.

She was undoubtedly one of the most inspirational people of her time. I hope that this book will keep her inspiration alive in the world, and that it will help you, the reader, to tap into your creative unconscious through dreams, just as Diana did.

Sweet dreams to you all – always!

'We must never stop dreaming. Dreams provide the nourishment for the soul, just as a meal does for the body. Many times in our lives we see our dreams shattered and our desires frustrated, but we have to continue dreaming. If we don't, our soul dies.'

PAULO COELHO, *THE PILGRIMAGE*